FOUNDATIONS
The Building Blocks for Understanding
Music Theory, Practicing & Playing

FOUNDATIONS

The Building Blocks for Understanding
Music Theory, Practicing & Playing

by Rick Alexander
Edited by Tara Alexander

3T Publishing, LLC
2026

3T PUBLISHING

ISBN 978-1-971161-00-6 (Paperback)
ISBN 978-1-971161-01-3 (EPUB)

Library of Congress Control Number: 2025927738

First Edition: 01-10-2026
Cover Design by Trinity Alexander
Edited by Tara Alexander

For permissions, licensing inquiries, or bulk educational use, please contact:
contact@3tpublishing.com

3T Publishing
Kenosha, WI 53142

Table of Contents

INTRODUCTION

Nothing will propel your musical ability more than an understanding of music theory.

I learned this the hard way. I've often been told I have an ear for music. I can hear something and generally figure out how to play it fairly quickly. The truth is, I can only do this because I've spent years picking up the guitar and exploring the neck, learning the nuances of the strings and the sounds they produce.

While this may sound like a good thing, in reality it held me back. Being able to rely on my ear allowed me to neglect the one thing I thought I didn't need: understanding why what I was playing sounded the way it did, music theory.

Once I began to understand the theory behind what I was playing, everything changed. I could learn songs more easily, enjoyed playing more deeply, and most importantly, began writing my own music with far less frustration. I no longer struggled to find the notes or chords I was hearing in my head.

I don't want to mislead you. Just as doctors are always practicing medicine, musicians are always practicing music. There is always more to learn and understand. As we progress in our musical journey, concepts that once felt difficult become second nature, and things that once felt impossible move within reach. This cycle is what drives us to practice and continue learning.

What you are about to read is a compilation of what I've learned over the years, presented in a way I hope is easy to read and, more importantly, easy to understand. My goal is to break music theory and its application into something practical, methodical, and real.

This book follows a foundational, building-block approach. Each section builds on the one before it, beginning with how we learn and why that matters, then using that understanding to establish a study and practice routine that sets you up for success.

With this foundation in place, you'll be prepared to explore music theory more confidently and discover what lies beneath the scales and chords you love, and how they work together to support one another.

Lastly, Chapter 7 contains worksheets designed to reinforce the material presented, allowing you to apply what you learn immediately.

If you want structured practice, here's where it lives.

Companion Workbook & Practice Resources (Optional)

Scan to learn more about the FOUNDATIONS Companion Workbook, designed to reinforce the concepts introduced in this book through structured, written practice.

Chapter 1: How to Study

Understanding How We Learn (and Why It Matters)

Most of us are never taught how to study effectively, we're simply told to memorize facts, figures, and formulas. This chapter explores the science of learning and offers practical strategies to avoid common study mistakes. Research shows we retain information best in focused 20-minute sessions, especially when we;

Read it, Write it, Speak it aloud and Repeat

Use this method along with the worksheets in Chapter 7 to actively engage with what you're learning.

Two Types of Memory

As musicians we use two types of memory when we play, declarative and procedural. Declarative memory allows us to recall the chords we want and procedural gives us the ability to physically play them. Working on these two together will make your playing fluent and natural. Think of those musician that make playing look so effortless. They put in the time required to be able to play without thinking first.

Declarative Memory

A type of long-term memory that involves conscious recollection of particular facts and events. Such as the names of scales, the positions of notes and the formulas. Think theory.

Procedural Memory

A type of long-term, implicit memory that allows you to automatically perform skills and actions without conscious thought or effort. Such as the muscle memory, finger positions, the physical playing of what you know.

Now that you understand how we best learn and retain information. You can structure your practice sessions accordingly.

Structuring Your Practice Sessions

Here's a structure that's worked for me:

5 Minutes: Review

Go over what you learned in your last session.
Read it. Write it. Say it out loud. Refresh your brain.

10 Minutes: Declarative Practice

This is mental work without your instrument.
Study the concept. Learn the shape, formula, or pattern. Study so that you can explain it out loud from memory.

10 Minutes: Procedural Practice

Pick up your instrument. Play slowly and deliberately. Focus on clean execution.
Start slow, once you can play it cleanly 3 times in a row, increase the speed and repeat.

Free Play: As Long As You Want

Now just play. Explore. Improvise. Enjoy your instrument. This is when creativity and inspiration happen.

How to Practice

Let's get real, practice is what makes the difference. Face it, most of us don't really understand or have clear direction of how to practice. That's why we end up stuck, repeating the same licks and struggling to improve.

Here's what I've learned (again, the hard way):

Set Your Intentions

Make a Schedule: Choose regular times that work for you and stick to them. Even short sessions done consistently will pay off.

Have a Purpose: Don't just pick up your instrument and noodle around. Know exactly what you want to work on and improve.

Stay Focused: Turn off distractions. Put your phone away. This is your time to improve.

Be Consistent: You won't see huge changes after one session, but you will after a period of consistent effort.

Practice! Practice! Practice!
What does this actually mean?

First Practice, Your Instrument

Practicing your instrument regularly, consistently, and with clear intent is essential because it builds muscle memory, strengthens technique, and deepens musical understanding. It turns effort into lasting progress and helps you grow from simply playing notes to truly making music.

Second Practice, Ear Training

Ear training is crucial. A well-trained ear helps you tighten your playing, understand what you're hearing, and unlocks the why behind the music you love. It's what lets you recognize chord progressions, play by ear, and really connect with music on a deeper level.

Third Practice, Music Theory

Understanding music theory and how it applies to your instrument changes the game. It helps you make sense of what you're doing and gives you a roadmap for exploring new music, playing with others, and writing your own music.

Putting It All Together

You can make progress by focusing on one area alone, but once you combine all three areas into your practicing and playing, you'll be amazed at how quickly things will change. Remember, too often we fall into habits causing us to practice the same things over and over. We keep hitting plateaus and wondering why we're stuck. The reason is simple: we're not practicing with purpose or focus. So Always, practice with intention, be consistent and don't get distracted.

How to Approach This Book

As I mentioned earlier, this book is designed in a building block approach, each concept building on the one before it. It's not meant to be rushed through. Take your time, use the practice sheets in chapter 7 to reinforce each chapter and ensure you really understand what you've learned before moving forward. With that being said,

Skim through the book to gain a general overview of what's ahead.

Then, go back and begin again with focus, reading and studying each section in order.

By the end, you'll be able to connect each chapter together and form the foundation you need to become the musician you want to be.

We've focused a lot on the how we learn and the path we're going to take on our journey to understand music theory. However, we can't overlook the importance of understanding the instrument you plan on applying this knowledge to.

Know Your Instrument

There's more to owning an instrument than just taking it out of its case, tuning it up, and playing. Learning proper setup and maintenance is vital to getting the most out of your playing. It allows you to know whether what you're hearing is a result of your technique or the limits of the instrument itself.

Knowing your instrument is critical to your development as a musician. By understanding the history of your instrument, how it's made, the materials it's made from, and how it all affects its playability and sound, will bring you closer to achieving the unique sound and playing style you're striving for.

Things like intonation, action (setup), and strings (size and brand) have a huge impact on your sound and how your instrument feels to play.

There was a time when I struggled to play chords up the neck. As I moved to different positions, the chords started to sound out of tune. I assumed it was my fingering. Eventually, I found out my guitar's intonation was off, and no matter how well I played, the chords would always sound out of tune. Once I got the intonation corrected, I could play a chord anywhere on the neck, and it sounded the way it should.

As you can see, it's vital you get to know your instrument. Know its strength and weaknesses. As you do, you'll build that relationship with it that only you'll have. Just as the great guitar players of our time have their number ones, you'll build a bond with yours and know without a doubt which instrument is meant to be your number one.

Before we close out this chapter on fundamentals, I believe it's important to cover music in general. We've all heard people say "That's not music! That's noise!" or something of the like. As we'll be discussing next, music is simply vibrations or sounds we like to hear together.

Music Explained

Let's keep this simple. Music is any combination of sounds you enjoy.

At its core, it's just vibrations. Arranged in a way that makes you feel something.

We'll touch on the basics of music theory and how they apply to the guitar and piano, but here's what I want you to remember above all:

If it sounds and feels good to you, it is.

Final Thoughts

This section was meant to be a guide for learning and practicing. In the end you need to find what works for you. Just keep in mind there is a science behind how we learn and retain information. Understand what it is you're trying to achieve and most importantly have fun.

You're not just learning music, you're learning how to think like a musician.

Chapter 2: Fundamentals

Sound is Vibrations

Sound is a vibration that travels through the air. When something shakes or moves quickly, like a guitar string, your voice, or a drum, it pushes the air around it. Those air waves reach your ears, and your brain hears it as sound.

Put your hand on your throat and hum. Do you feel that buzzing? That's your vocal cords vibrating to make sound!

Pitch: High vs. Low

The term *pitch* is used to help define how high or low a vibrations tonal sound is. The faster something vibrates, the higher the pitch, the higher the tonal sound, like a bird. The opposite goes for slower vibrations. The slower something vibrates, the lower the pitch, the lower the vibrations tonal sound is. Like the strings of a bass guitar.

Pitch: Used to describe how high or low a sound is.

High Pitch = Fast vibrations (like a bird or a whistle)

Low Pitch = Slow vibrations (like thunder or a tuba)

Notes: Assigning Note Values to a Pitch

In music, the first seven letters of the English alphabet are used in sequence to assign a note value to the various pitches used in music. These letters are called notes A, B, C, D, E, F, G. Notes that do not have an accidental, such as these, are called *Natural Notes*. More on accidentals shortly.

The Musical Alphabet: A–G

The human ear can hear more than seven pitch tones, yet only the letters A through G are used to identify them. As a pitch rises or falls, this sequence of letters repeats in the same order. The pattern itself never changes, it just cycles continuously.

For example, if we start on the note 'A' and move upward in pitch to 'G', the notes would be A, B, C, D, E, F, G. If we continue higher in pitch beyond 'G', the sequence starts over again from 'A' and repeats: A, B, C, D, E, F, G, A, B, C, D, E, F... This pattern remains the same no matter which note you start on, and it works the same way when moving downward in pitch as well

...C, D, E, F, G, A, B, C, D, E, F, G, A, B, C, D, E, F, G, A, B, C, D, E, F, G, A, B, C, D, E, F, G...

Octaves

An *Octave* occurs when two notes share the same name but are higher or lower in pitch from each other. Figure 1 below shows three 'E' notes shown in an extended version of the musical alphabet. These notes represent three octaves, different pitches, of the note 'E'.

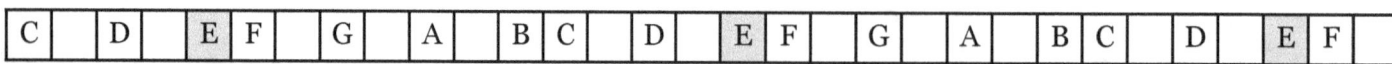

Figure 1: Demonstrates three octaves of the note "E"

Accidentals

Accidentals are symbols in music that tell us to alter a notes pitch. There are three accidentals you'll see most often when reading music, Sharps (#), Flats (b) and Naturals (♮).

A **Sharp (#)** raises a note by a half step: it makes the note one step higher. Think of it like walking up a flight of stairs, the step above is a pitch higher than the one you're on.

A **Flat (b)** lowers a note by a half step: it makes the note a step lower. Again, stepping down a stair lowers the pitch.

A **Natural (♮)** Cancels a sharp or flat: It returns the note to its original, natural pitch. It restores the note to its "default" sound, resetting it back to where it started.

When needed, you can double a sharp or a flat. Doubling either of these raises or lowers the note by a whole tone 'two semitones'. As you would expect, the name for this is called a *Double Sharp* or *Double Flat*.

Sharp	Double Sharp	Flat	Double Flat	Natural
♯	𝄪	♭	♭♭	♮

Figure 2: Accidentals

Let's Review:
Sound: is a vibration.
Pitch: defines how high or low a vibration is or sounds.
Notes: are used to name a pitch.
The Musical Alphabet: the first seven letters of the alphabet 'A, B, C, D, E, F, G' are used as notes to name a pitch. The Sequence of letters never change they just repeat.
Natural Notes: are the notes of the musical alphabet without accidentals.
An Octave: is the same note played at a higher or lower pitch.
Accidentals: are symbols in music that tell us to alter the pitch of a note.
A Sharp: Raises the pitch of a note by a half step.
A Flat: Lowers the pitch of a note by a half step.
A Natural: Returns a note to its natural pitch.

Now that you have the foundation of the musical language, we'll move on to how we read and write music. As we move through the chapters and sub sections, you'll be introduced to terms that have yet to be covered. When this occurs we'll provide a general understanding of the term to get you through the section, but don't worry, it will be covered in greater detail later as you progress. It may seem that some topics are repeated, this is intentional. Keep in mind you are given the information you need at the time you need it and reinforcing it where it applies. Again the foundations.

Chapter 3: Reading and Writing Music

The Musical Staff

The foundation of music notation begins with the *Staff*. The plural of staff is *staves*. A Staff is a set of five horizontal lines and four spaces in which musical notes are placed. The placement of notes on the staff tells us the notes pitch. Understanding the staves is essential for reading and writing music.

The Staff: The staff consists of five horizontal lines with four spaces between them.
Lines and Spaces: Each line and space represent a specific pitch. Notes can be placed on both lines and spaces.

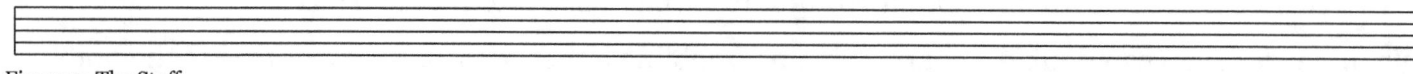

Figure 3: The Staff

Ledger lines extend the staff beyond its original five lines and four spaces. They allow for the notation of notes outside the original range of the staff. Ledger lines are short horizontal lines placed above or below the staff to extend its range.

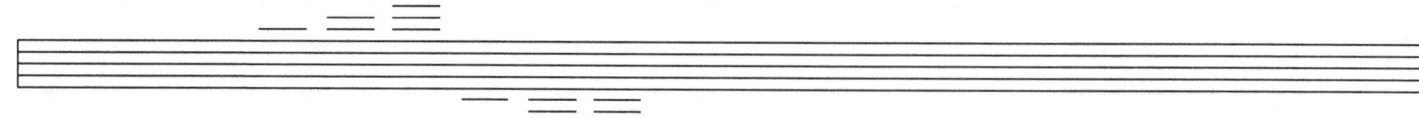

Figure 4: Ledger Lines

How They Work: Each additional line or space above or below the staff represents an additional pitch extending the sequence of notes in that direction.

Placement of Notes: Notes can be placed either on the ledger line or in the space above or below.

Where Used: Ledger lines are used with all staves.

Clefs

A *clef* is a symbol placed at the beginning of the staff that indicates which pitch (note value) the lines and spaces represent. It provides context for how the notes on the staff should be interpreted. We'll be focusing on the two most commonly used, *Treble Clef* and *Bass Clef*.

TREBLE CLEF

BASS CLEF

Figure 5: The Treble & Bass Clefs

Treble Clef: Used for higher-pitched instruments like the guitar, violin, flute, and trumpet.
Bass Clef: Used for lower-pitched instruments like the cello, bass guitar, and tuba.

Treble Clef (G Clef)

The *treble clef* assigns the note 'G' to the second line of the staff. The 'G Clef' name comes from the fact the lower loop of the clef wraps around the 'G' line/note on the staff.

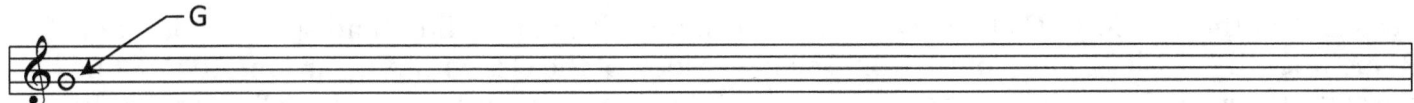

Figure 6: The Treble Clef

Bass Clef (F Clef)

The *bass clef* assigns the note 'F' to the fourth line of the staff. The name 'F Clef' comes from the two dots of the clef encasing the 'F' line of the staff.

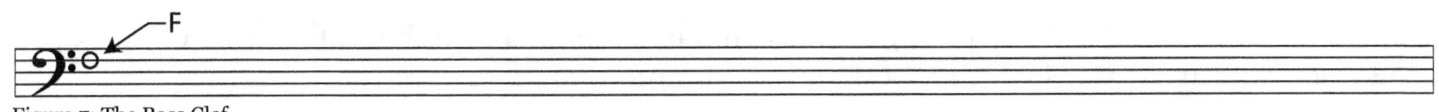

Figure 7: The Bass Clef

The Grand Staff

The *grand staff* is a set of two staves joined together to show a wide range of pitches, most often used for keyboard instruments like the piano. The treble clef is placed on the upper staff and the bass clef on the lower staff, allowing notes for the right hand and left hand to be written clearly. At the far left, a brace curves around both staves to connect them, indicating that they are read and performed as one system rather than two separate lines of music.

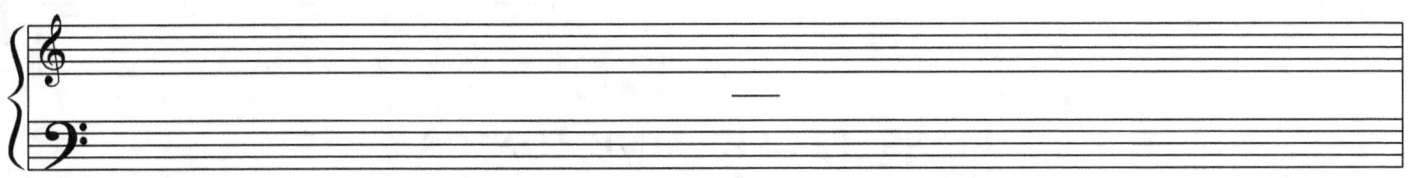

Figure 8: The Grand Staff

Let's Review:
The Staff: is comprised of five (5) lines and four (4) spaces.
Ledger Lines: are used to extend a staff up or down. (Higher or Lower Notes)
Clef: are used to assign notes values (Letters) to the lines and spaces of a staff.
Treble Clef: indicates the second line of the staff represents the note G above middle C.
Bass Clef: indicates the fourth line of the staff represents the note F below middle C.
The Grand Staff: Consists of both the treble and bass clef staves.

Notes of the Staves

Each line and space are assigned a *note value* (letter) from the musical alphabet. Remember the sequence of letters A through G that repeat. These note values are assigned vertically across the staff by the Clef at the beginning of the staff.

Let's look at the Treble 'G' Clef and how it assigns note values to the lines and spaces of its staff. Remember the 'G Clef' name comes from the lower loop of the clef wrapping around the 'G' line on the staff. If we lay the alphabet vertically on top of the lines and spaces with the 'G' on top of the second line, the other lines and spaces get their note identifier.

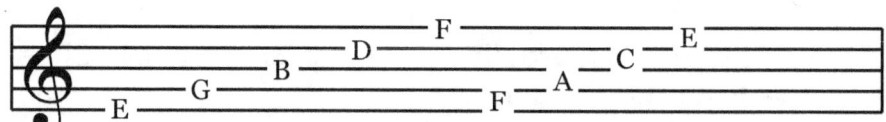

Figure 9: Notes of the Staff

Understanding how to read and write the notes on the staff without thinking about them, just as we read words on a page, is essential for both musicians and composers.

Notes of the Staves and Mnemonics

Mnemonics are used to help us remember the names of the lines and spaces when first starting out. When reading the notes of the staff, the notes are read vertically from bottom to the top.

TREBLE (G) CLEF MNEMONICS

Lines: "Every Good Boy Does Fine" (E, G, B, D, F)

Spaces: "F A C E" (F, A, C, E)

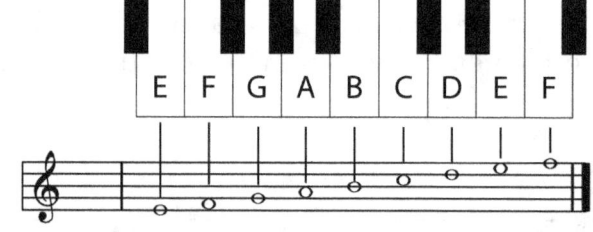

Figure 10: Notes on the treble staff

BASS (F) CLEF MNEMONICS

Lines: "Good Boys Do Fine Always" (G, B, D, F, A)

Spaces: "All Cows Eat Grass" (A, C, E, G)

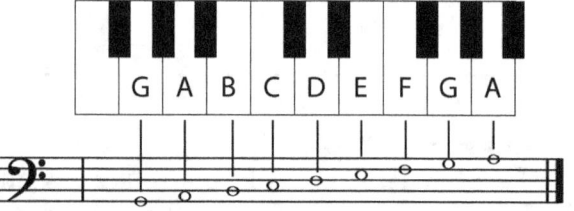

Figure 11: Notes on the bass staff

Let's Review:
Lines & Spaces: are assigned a note value based on the Clef on the staff.
Note Values: are named after the first seven letters of the alphabet: A, B, C, D, E, F, G.
Mnemonics: are used to remember line note values of the treble and bass clef.

Key Signature

In music, when someone speaks of the "Key" of a song, they are referring to what scale the song is written in. It tells the musician which notes are constantly altered (sharp or flat) throughout the song.

A *Key Signature* is used at the beginning of the staff to visually represent the Key of the song. It makes it easier to read and write music without needing to mark every altered note individually.

Example: The key of "G Major" has a single sharp placed on the 'F' line of the staff. This lets the musician know that throughout the song every time an "F Note" is noted it is to be played as an 'F#'.

G Major

Figure 12: G Major Key Signature

There are 15 major key signatures. The key of C major has no sharps or flats. The other 14 key signatures have between 1 to 7 sharps or 1 to 7 flats. Each Major Key Signature also represents a natural minor. This will be discussed further when we learn about scales.

Figure 13: Major Key Signatures

Time Signature

Time signatures indicate how many beats are in each measure and what type of note gets the beat. It appears at the beginning of a piece of music, right after the clef and key signature.

Top Number: Number of beats per measure.
Bottom Number: Type of note that gets one beat (e.g., 4 = quarter note, 8 = eighth note).
Common Time (4/4): This is the most common time signature in Western music, meaning four beats per measure, and the quarter note gets one beat.
Other Time Signatures: 3/4 (three beats per measure, quarter note gets one beat), 6/8 (six beats per measure, eighth note gets one beat), etc.

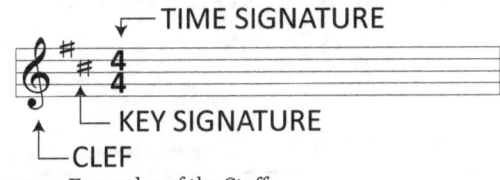
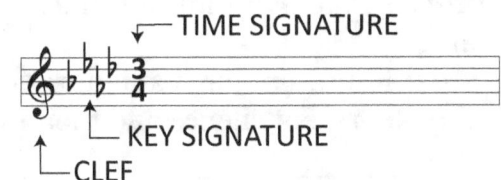

Figure 14: Examples of the Staff

Bar Lines and Measures

Bar lines are vertical black lines that divide the staff into measures. The number of beats in a measure are dictated by the Time Signature we just discussed.

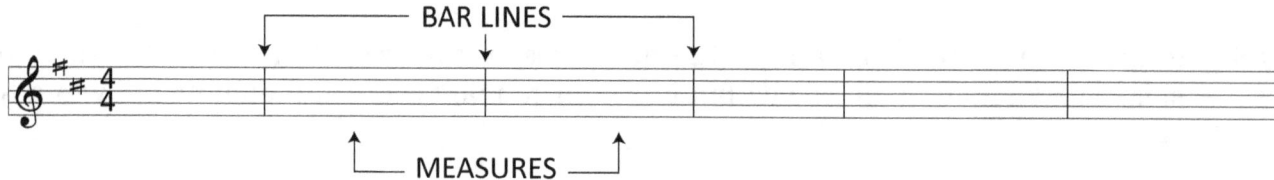

Figure 15: Bar Lines & Measures on the Staff

Notes and Rests: Sound and Silence

Notes and *rests* are symbols that show when sound happens and when silence is held. A note represents a sound, a specific pitch, with its shape showing how long that sound should last, while a rest represents silence. For example, whole, half, quarter, eighth, and sixteenth notes each have matching rests that mark equal durations of silence. Together, notes and rests create the rhythm of music, telling us not just which pitch to play, but also how long to play it or when to be silent, giving music its flow and structure.

NAME	NOTE	REST	BEATS	NOTES PER $\frac{4}{4}$ MEASURE
WHOLE			4	
HALF			2	
QUARTER			1	
EIGHT			1/2	
SIXTEENTH			1/4	

Figure 16: Note Duration Chart (4/4 Time)

Let's Review:
Clefs: Assigns note values to the lines and spaces of the staff.
Key Signature: Indicate the key to the music, showing which notes are consistently sharp or flat throughout the piece.
Time Signature: Indicates the number of beats per measure and which note value gets one beat.
Notes: Represent pitch and duration of the sound.
Rest: Represent silence and their duration.

Elements of the Staves

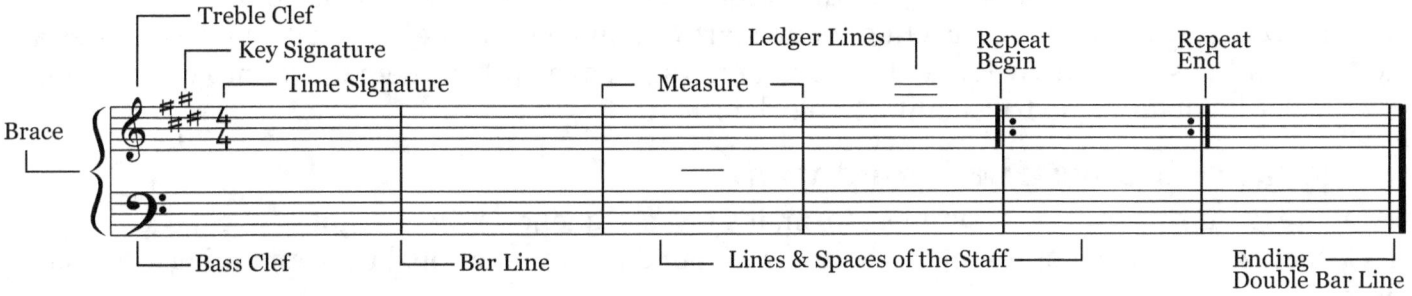

Notes of the Grand Staff

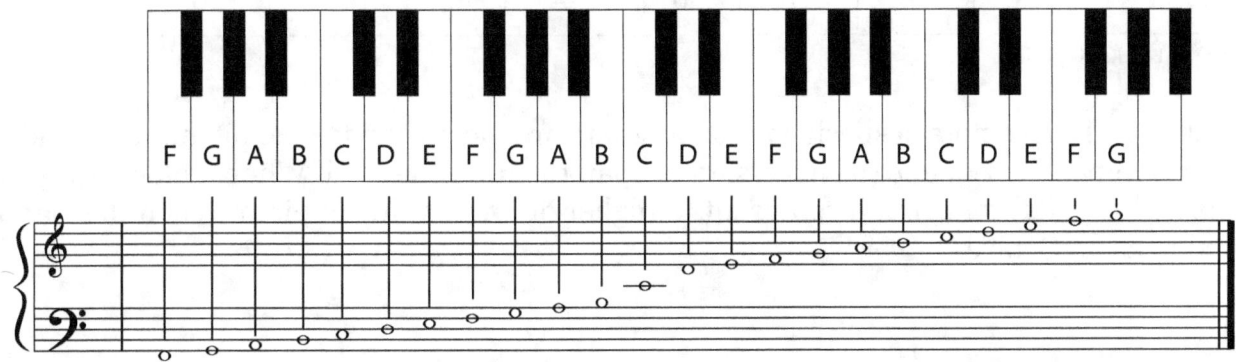

Time Signatures

| Four beats per measure.
Quarter note receives one beat. | Three beats per measure.
Quarter note receives one beat. | Two beats per measure.
Quarter note receives one beat. | Six beats per measure.
Eighth note receives one beat. |

Note	Name	Rest	Beats	Notes per 4/4 Measure
𝅝	**Whole**		4	𝅝
𝅗𝅥	**Half**		2	𝅗𝅥 𝅗𝅥
𝅘𝅥	**Quarter**		1	𝅘𝅥 𝅘𝅥 𝅘𝅥 𝅘𝅥
𝅘𝅥𝅮	**Eighth**		1/2	𝅘𝅥𝅮𝅘𝅥𝅮𝅘𝅥𝅮𝅘𝅥𝅮 𝅘𝅥𝅮𝅘𝅥𝅮𝅘𝅥𝅮𝅘𝅥𝅮
𝅘𝅥𝅯	**Sixteenth**		1/4	𝅘𝅥𝅯𝅘𝅥𝅯𝅘𝅥𝅯𝅘𝅥𝅯 𝅘𝅥𝅯𝅘𝅥𝅯𝅘𝅥𝅯𝅘𝅥𝅯 𝅘𝅥𝅯𝅘𝅥𝅯𝅘𝅥𝅯𝅘𝅥𝅯 𝅘𝅥𝅯𝅘𝅥𝅯𝅘𝅥𝅯𝅘𝅥𝅯

Figure 17: Reading & Writing Music Visual Overview

Chapter 4: Introduction to Music Theory

When it comes to *music theory*, there are endless books, videos, and courses on the subject. You can fall down an endless rabbit hole on your quest for understanding. This book is not meant to be an in-depth course, but rather an introduction to start you on your journey. I've taken my struggles and the "Why didn't someone say it like that!" moments and have broken them down into what I hope is an easy-to-understand, no frills, building block format.

12 Blocks of Music: The Foundation

If you break music down to its simplest form, it's just a sequence of twelve notes. We'll use the blocks below to visually represent the notes as we build our foundational understanding of music theory.

1	2	3	4	5	6	7	8	9	10	11	12

Figure 18: The 12 Blocks of Music

Each block represents a note, a specific pitch. As there are more than twelve pitches of sound, the twelve blocks repeat in sequence as necessary to span the range needed. When a block is repeated, it retains its identity, its name, but it represents a higher or lower value of pitch. When this happens, it is referred to as an Octave.

Octaves

An *octave* is when two blocks, or notes, share the same name but are either higher or lower in pitch. To be specific, an octave spans twelve semitones (explained next) in either direction from the original note.

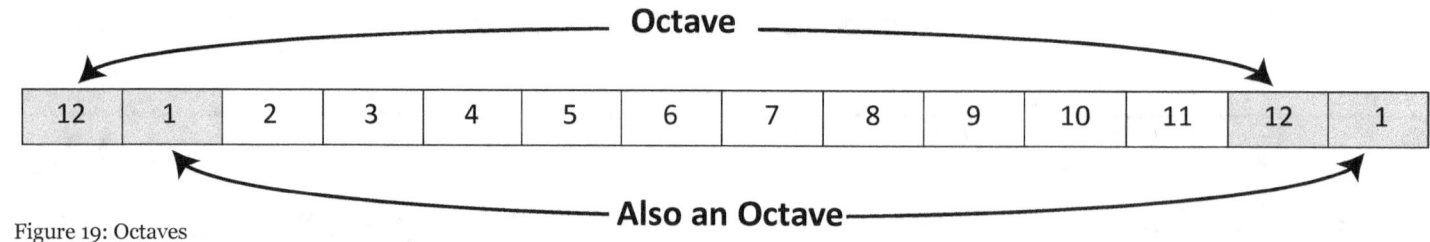

Figure 19: Octaves

Interval, Semitone and Tone

To understand how music works, we need to understand how the blocks/notes relate to each other in pitch. That's where intervals, semitones and tones come in. They're the foundation of scales, chords, and melodies. Let's break each one down:

Interval

An *interval* is the distance between two block/notes. Intervals are measured in semitones. They define how notes relate to each other. This interval relationship gives music its character and emotional quality.

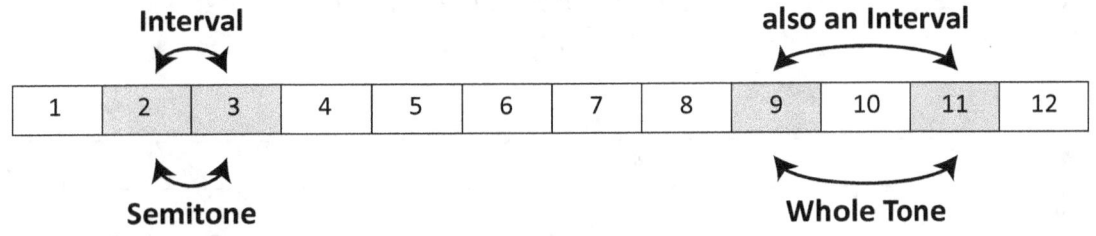

Figure 20: Intervals & Tones

Semitone (Half Step)

A *semitone*, also called a half step, is the smallest interval, distance, between two notes. In the 12-note system moving up or down by one semitone means going from one block to the next. If you're on block 2, a semitone up is block 3, a semitone down is block 1.

Tone (Whole Step)

A *tone*, also called a whole step, is made up of two semitones. If starting on block 9, moving up a tone takes you to block 11, while moving down a tone takes you to block 7.

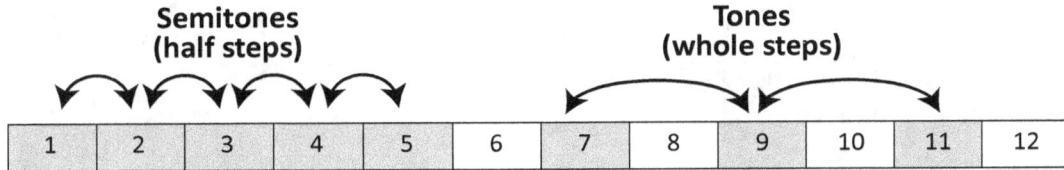

Figure 21: Tones & Semitones

<u>**Let's Review:**</u>
12 Notes/Block: Music is a sequence of twelve (12) blocks/notes that repeat in sequence up and down the musical ladder at different octaves.
Octave: An octave is the same two blocks/notes that are twelve semitones apart.
Interval: Is the distance between two notes. Intervals are measured in semitones.
Semitone: A semitone (or half step) is the smallest possible interval between two notes.
Tone: A tone (or whole step) is an interval that spans two semitones.

Musical Alphabet

Now that we've covered the twelve repeating blocks in music, let's connect them to the musical alphabet. As discussed in chapter 3, the alphabet uses the letters A through G, called the natural notes, which form the foundation of music.

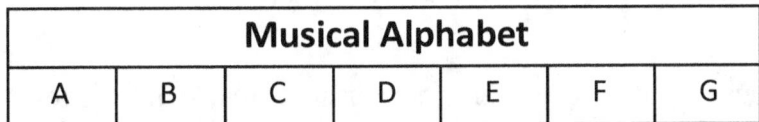

Figure 22: The musical Alphabet

As there are seven letters and twelve total block/notes, the remaining five blocks are identified by adding accidentals called, sharps (#) and flats (♭), to the natural notes.

12 Blocks	1	2	3	4	5	6	7	8	9	10	11	12
Musical Alphabet	C	#/♭	D	#/♭	E	F	#/♭	G	#/♭	A	#/♭	B

Figure 23: 12 Blocks with Musical Alphabet

The way these twelve notes are spaced out using half steps (semitones) and whole steps (whole tones) can be seen clearly on the piano keys, it's like a musical map. The white keys represent the Natural Notes 'A,B,C,D,E,F,G' and the black keys are the Sharps (#) and Flats (♭).

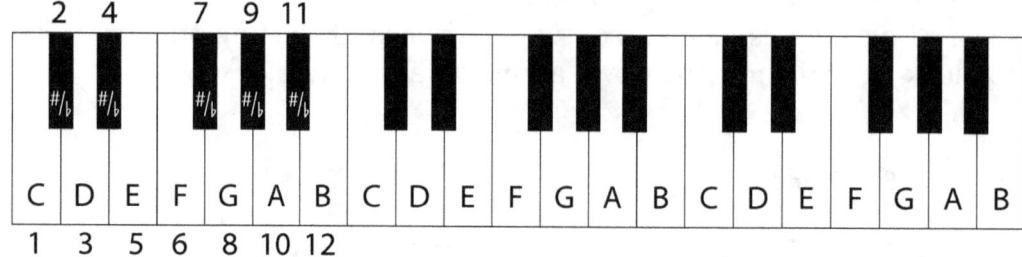

Figure 24: Notes on the Piano

The piano's clear and linear layout makes it an ideal instrument for learning music theory, especially for beginners. Each pitch appears in only one place across the keys on the piano, providing a visually straightforward way to understand pitch relationships, scales, and intervals. In contrast, the guitar has the same pitch in multiple locations across different strings and frets, which can make pitch mapping more complex.

The example below shows how the same 'E' pitch can be found in three different location along the guitar fretboard.

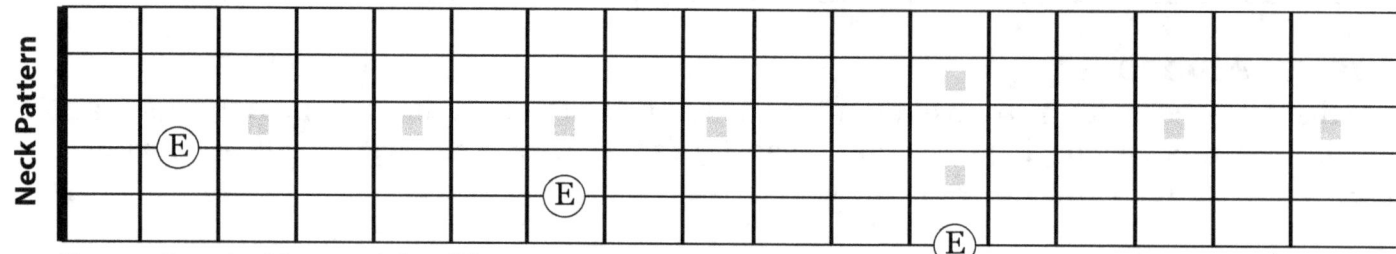

Figure 25: Example of the same pitch on different strings & frets on a guitar neck

Guitar players use shapes or patterns to help memorize notes, scales, intervals and chords across the fretboard.

Sharps (#) & Flats (b)

When a *sharp* or *flat* is placed next to a note, the sharp (#) raises the pitch of the note by a semitone (half step), and a flat (♭) lowers the pitch of a note by a semitone (half step).

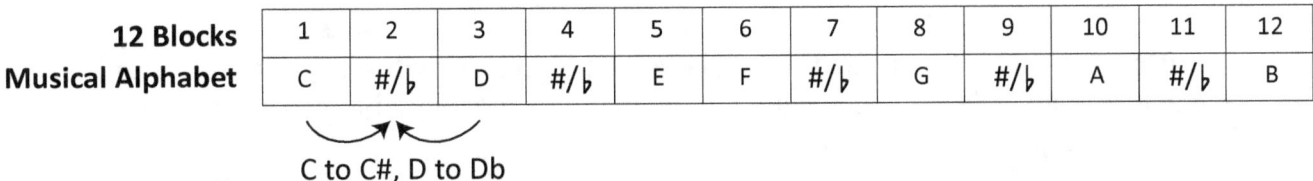

12 Blocks	1	2	3	4	5	6	7	8	9	10	11	12
Musical Alphabet	C	#/♭	D	#/♭	E	F	#/♭	G	#/♭	A	#/♭	B

C to C#, D to Db

Figure 26: The 12 Blocks with Accidentals

Now, you might wonder: When is a note sharp or flat? We'll explore that in more detail later. For now, all you need to know is that a sharp raises a note's pitch, and a flat lowers it.

Enharmonic

When two notes have the same pitch but are written in different musical contexts, such as a C# and Db, they are called *enharmonic*. Sharps and flats have enharmonic equivalents, notes that sound the same but are spelled with a different name.

For example, C# and Db have the same pitch, however it is the musical context that determines it name. Similarly, F# and Gb are the same pitch, but their spelling changes based on the scale or key they are in. We will cover what makes a note sharp or flat in more detail as we get further into scales.

Let's Review:
Musical Alphabet: The musical alphabet consists of seven letters (notes): A through G.
Natural Notes: are notes that do not have an accidental.
Sharp (#): A sharp raises the pitch of a note by a semitone (half step).
Flat (♭): A flat lowers the pitch of a note by a semitone (half step).
Enharmonic: Enharmonic notes are two notes that are written in different musical contexts, but have the same pitch.

Scales

A *musical scale* is a sequence of notes that follows a specific pattern of intervals. Scales form the foundation of melody, harmony, and most musical compositions, providing the tonal framework for music.

Scales help define the key of a piece of music (Review Key Signatures) and shape how the melody and harmony are structured. Each type of scale has its own unique pattern of intervals, which gives it a distinct sound or emotional quality. These interval patterns repeat across octaves, just like the notes themselves.

Key Characteristics of a Scale

Notes: A scale consists of a series of notes, typically within one octave, although some scales can span multiple octaves.

Tonality: Most scales are based on a specific tonic (or "root note"), which gives the scale its identity.

The *chromatic scale*, is a scale that includes all twelve pitches, each a semitone (half step) apart. It is the most basic and complete scale because it covers all of the available pitches within an octave, without focusing on a particular key or tonality.

12 Blocks	1	2	3	4	5	6	7	8	9	10	11	12
Chromatic Scale	C	C#/Db	D	D#/Eb	E	F	F#/Gb	G	G#/Ab	A	A#/Bb	B

Figure 27: The 12 Blocks with the Chromatic Scale

At this point, it's important to clarify that the numbers we use to refer to the twelve blocks are not tied to the letters or notes themselves. As we explore scales more deeply and learn how they are built, we'll see that numbers are related to degrees of the scale, not the specific name or letter of the note.

Tonic vs. Root Note

The *tonic* is the first note of a scale and acts as the tonal center or "home" note. It provides a sense of resolution and stability in music, often being the note that melodies and harmonies resolve to, especially at the end of phrases or at the conclusion of a piece. The tonic defines the key of the music.

The *root note*, on the other hand, is the foundational note of a chord and determines the chord's name. The tonic and root note are not always identical. The tonic refers specifically to the first note of the scale and governs the key, whereas the root note is tied to individual chords and can appear in different positions within a chord (such as in chord inversions).

Let's Review:
A Scale: is a sequence of notes arranged in ascending or descending order of pitch, following a specific pattern of intervals.
Tonality: Scales are based on a specific tonic, or "root note," which gives the scale its identity.
Chromatic Scale: A scale that includes all 12 notes within an octave, each a semitone apart.
Tonic Note: The tonic is the first note of a scale and serves as the "home" note of the key.
Root Note: The root note is the foundational note of a chord and gives the chord its name.

Chapter 5: Theory Applied-Scales

In this chapter, we'll focus on the foundational building blocks of scales, the notes within a scale, intervals, major and minor scale structures, degrees and modes. You'll learn how to build and analyze scales, which are the foundation for understanding harmony, melody, and the overall structure of music.

This chapter will set the stage for later explorations of how scales are used to construct chords. By the end, you'll have a solid understanding of how scales form the backbone of musical composition and provide the emotional quality of a melody.

Building Scales: The Notes within a Scale

Building a scale starts with selecting a note, the tonic note. Then using intervals that provide specific emotional qualities to select subsequent notes. The number of notes within a scale can vary. The major and minor scales, consist of seven notes, while the pentatonic only has five. By adjusting the number of notes and the intervals between them, you can create different types of scales with different emotional qualities.

Intervals: Building Upon the Foundation

Understanding intervals is essential to understanding a scales emotional sounding quality. Intervals describe the distance between two notes. They help us analyze and describe scales, chords, progressions and their emotional qualities.

An interval that is within a single octave is called a *Simple Interval*. An interval that spans more than one octave is called a *Compound Interval*.

Each interval has a specific name based on its number of steps from one note to another and its sound quality. These are major, minor, perfect, augmented, or diminished. Below is a breakdown of the different types of intervals:

Perfect Intervals: Unison (P1), Fourth (P4), Fifth (P5), Octave (P8).
- An interval is Perfect when it sounds stable, complete, forming the purest consonances.
- The quality of a Perfect interval can only be changed to Augmented, or Diminished, Never Major or Minor.
- Raising a Perfect interval by a Semitone changes its quality to *Augmented*.
- Lowering a Perfect interval by a Semitone changes its quality to *Diminished*.

Major Intervals: 2nd (M2), 3rd (M3), 6th (M6), 7th (M7).
- An interval is Major when it is a whole step larger than its minor counterpart, giving a bright and open sound.
- A Major intervals quality can be changed to Minor, Augmented and Diminished.
- Raising a Major interval by a Semitone changes its quality to *Augmented*.
- Lowering a Major interval by a Semitone changes its quality to *Minor*.
- Lowering a Major interval by a Tone changes its quality to *Diminished*.

Minor Intervals: 2nd (m2), 3rd (m3), 6th (m6), 7th (m7).

- An interval is Minor when it is a half step smaller than its major form, creating a darker or more tense sound.
- A Minor intervals quality can be changed to Major, Augmented and Diminished.
- Raising a Minor interval by a Semitone changes its quality to *Major*.
- Raising a Minor interval by a Tone changes its quality to *Augmented*.
- Lowering a Minor interval by a Semitone changes its quality to *Diminished*.

Augmented Intervals:

- An interval is Augmented when it is a half step larger than either a perfect or major interval, giving it an expanded, stretched quality.
- Augmented intervals are one semitone larger than its Major or Perfect equivalent.
- An Augmented intervals quality can be changed to Perfect, Major, Minor, and Diminished.
- Lowering an Augmented interval by a Semitone changes its quality to *Major* or *Perfect*.
- Lowering an Augmented interval by a Tone changes its quality to *Minor* or *Diminished*.
- Lowering an Augmented interval by a 3 Semitones changes its quality to *Diminished*.

Diminished Intervals:

- An interval is Diminished when it is a half step smaller than either a perfect or minor interval, producing the most compressed and tense sound.
- Diminished intervals are one semitone smaller than Minor or Perfect intervals.
- A Diminished intervals quality can be changed to Perfect, Major, Minor, and Augmented.
- Raising a Diminished interval by a Semitone changes its quality to *Minor*.
- Raising a Diminished interval by a Tone changes its quality to *Major*.
- Raising a Diminished interval by a 3 Semitone changes its quality to *Augmented*.

In music theory, the use of capitalization and lowercase in interval abbreviations is important because it clearly distinguishes between different qualities of intervals. A capital 'M' indicates a major interval, while a lowercase 'm' represents a minor interval; confusing the two changes the meaning entirely. Similarly, a capital 'P' is used for perfect intervals, a capital 'A' is used for augmented intervals, and a lower case 'd' is used for diminished. Without this careful use of capitalization, interval names can easily be misread, leading to mistakes in analysis, performance, and understanding of music.

Interval Chart

Interval Name	Semitones	Interval Abreviation
Unison	0	P1
Minor 2nd	1	m2
Major 2nd	2	M2
Minor 3rd	3	m3
Major 3rd	4	M3
Diminished 4th	4	d4
Perfect 4th	5	P4
Augmented 4th	6	A4
Diminished 5th	6	d5
Perfect 5th	7	P5
Augmented 5th	8	A5
Minor 6th	8	m6
Major 6th	9	M6
Diminished 7th	9	d7
Minor 7th	10	m7
Major 7th	11	M7
Octave	12	P8

Figure 28: Interval Chart

Intervals on the Staff

Being able to visually identify intervals on the staff quickly is essential. The graphic below shows intervals as they appear on the staff, starting with unison, the same note repeated, and moving up to its octave. This visual guide highlights the spacing and placement of notes in written music. As we continue, we'll also examine these intervals on the piano and guitar to build a well-rounded understanding across instruments. While shown in sequence here, intervals can also appear stacked vertically, forming chords.

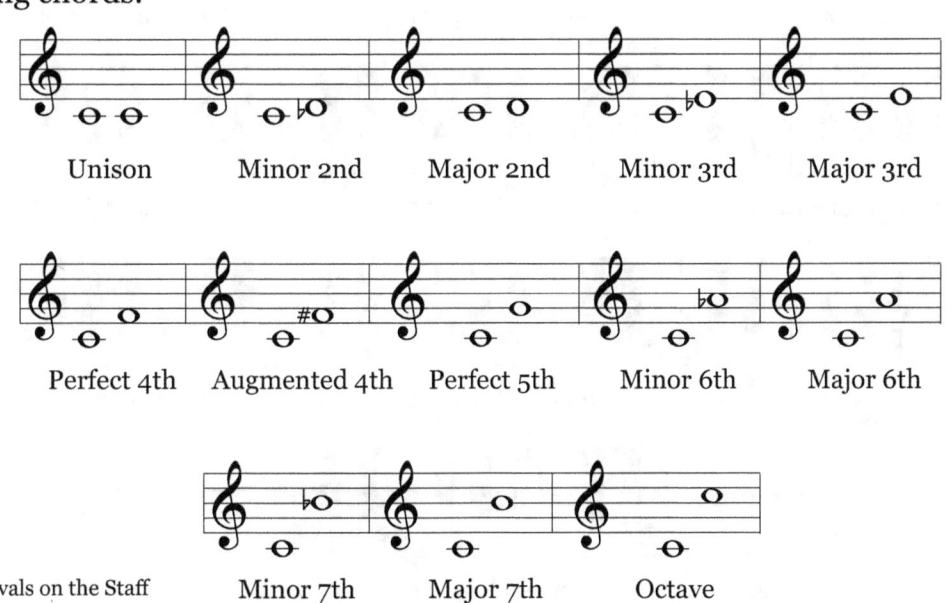

Figure 29: Intervals on the Staff

Unison · Minor 2nd · Major 2nd · Minor 3rd · Major 3rd

Perfect 4th · Augmented 4th · Perfect 5th · Minor 6th · Major 6th

Minor 7th · Major 7th · Octave

Recognizing intervals on the staff is essential for reading music fluently. As you become familiar with the way each interval looks, you'll start to see patterns in melodies and harmonies that make reading and writing music easier.

Let's Review:
Intervals: Intervals are measured in semitones.
Perfect Intervals: Unison (P1), Fourth (P4), Fifth (P5), Octave (P8).
Major Intervals: 2nd (M2), 3rd (M3), 6th (M6), 7th (M7).
Minor Intervals: 2nd (m2), 3rd (m3), 6th (m6), 7th (m7).
Augmented Intervals: are one semitone larger than its Major or Perfect equivalent.
Diminished Intervals: are one semitone smaller than a Minor or Perfect intervals.
Simple Interval: is an interval that spans within a single octave .
Compound Interval: is an interval that spans more than one octave.

Intervals on the Piano

On the piano, intervals can easily be seen through the layout of the keys. The graphic below illustrates each interval from unison to octave as they appear on the keyboard. Starting from a single note then showing its partner note for each interval. You'll notice that some intervals span only white keys, while others include black keys. This reflects both the distance and pitch relationship between notes. Understanding how intervals look and sound on the piano will strengthen your ear and help you navigate the keyboard with confidence.

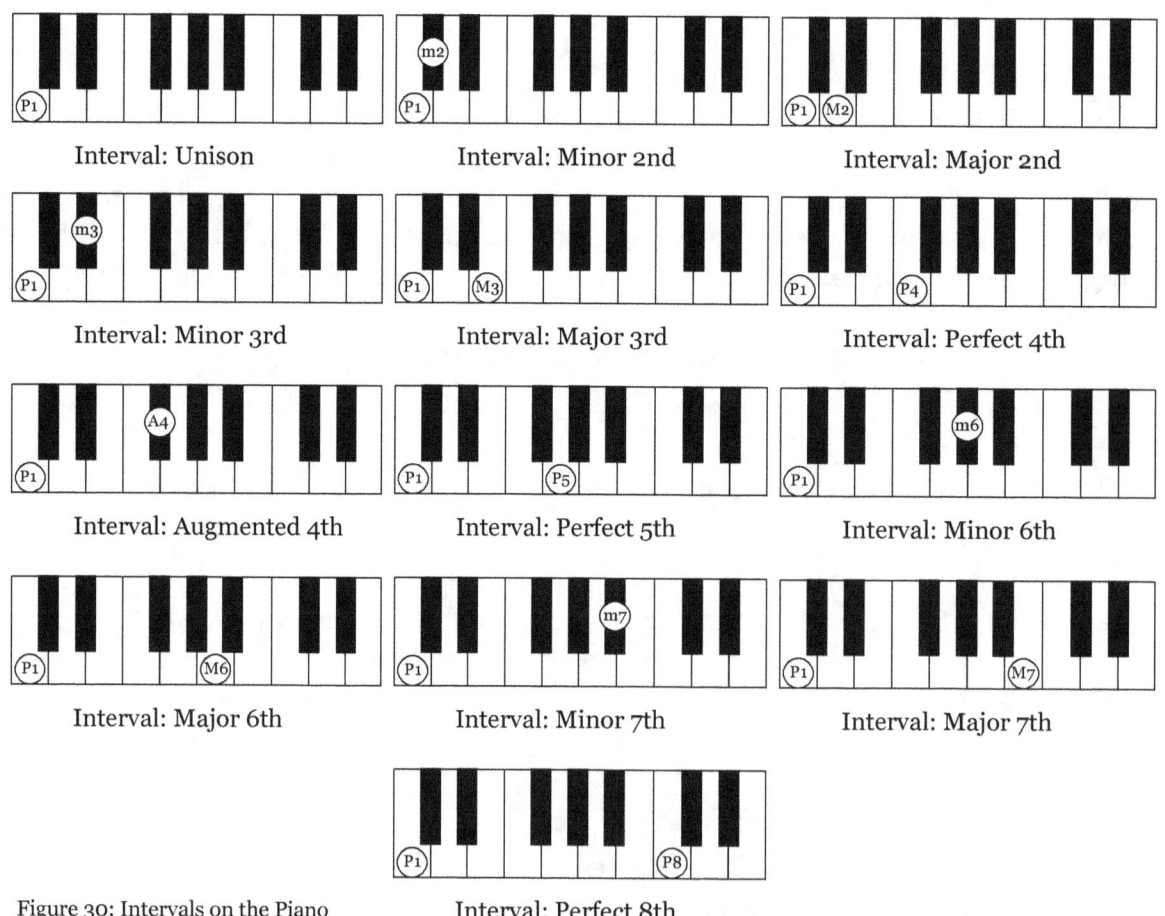

Interval: Unison   Interval: Minor 2nd   Interval: Major 2nd

Interval: Minor 3rd   Interval: Major 3rd   Interval: Perfect 4th

Interval: Augmented 4th   Interval: Perfect 5th   Interval: Minor 6th

Interval: Major 6th   Interval: Minor 7th   Interval: Major 7th

Figure 30: Intervals on the Piano   Interval: Perfect 8th

Understanding how intervals appear on the piano helps build a strong connection between your ear and your hands. These patterns are the foundation for scales, chords, and improvisation, so take time to explore and internalize each one.

Intervals on the Guitar

On the guitar, intervals take on a different visual and physical shape across the fretboard. The graphic below shows each interval from unison to octave, using the same starting note and displaying how far and in what direction each interval is found. Unlike the piano, the same interval can often be played in multiple locations on the guitar, which makes learning their shapes especially valuable. Recognizing these interval patterns will help you better understand chord construction, scales, and soloing across the neck.

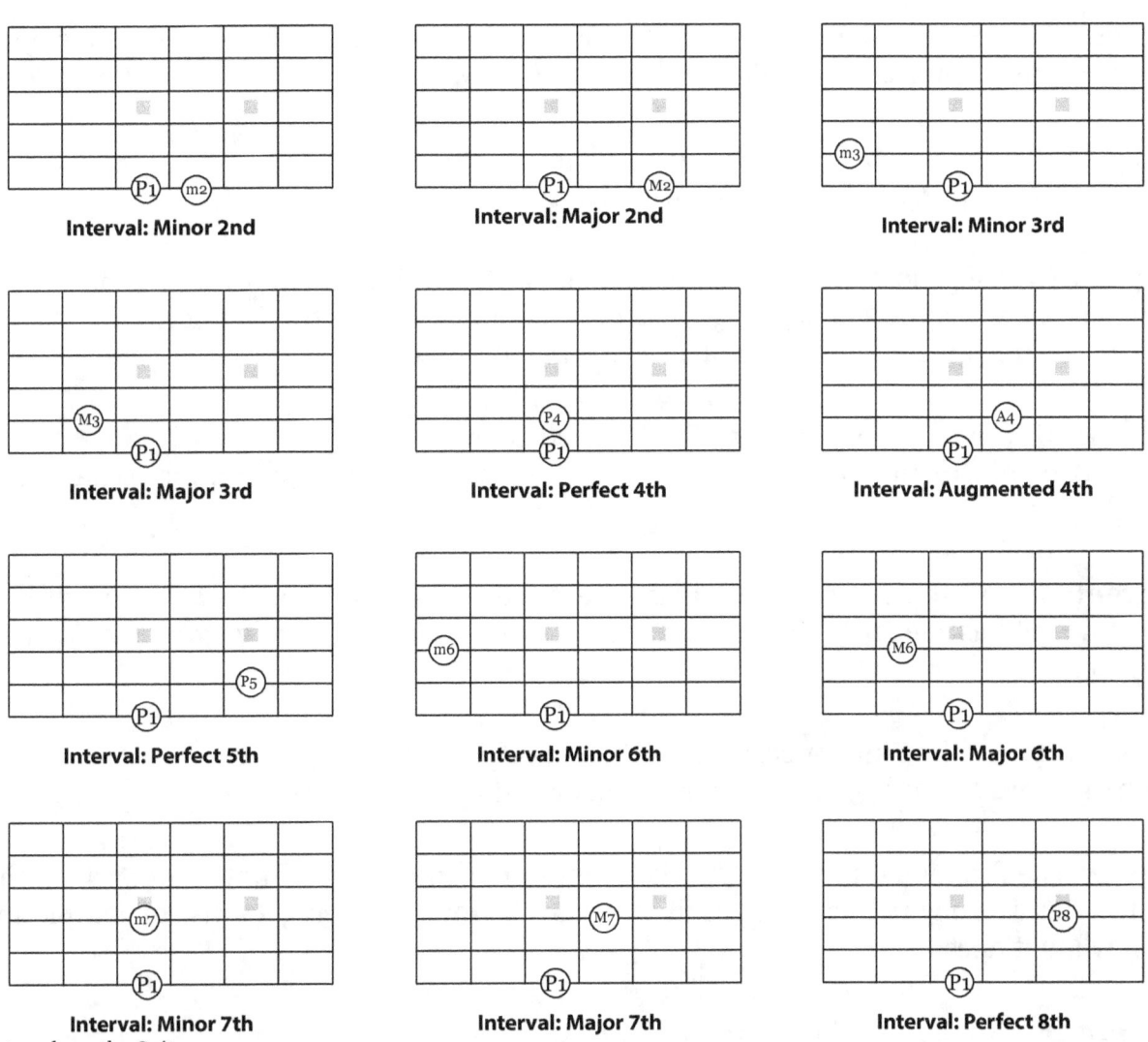

Figure 31: Intervals on the Guitar

Learning interval shapes on the guitar fretboard is key to mastering the instrument. These patterns repeat across the neck, making it easier to find chords, scales, and melodies in any position. The more you recognize them, the more freely you'll be able to play.

Degrees of a Scale

Degrees refer to the specific position of a note within a scale. Each note in a scale is assigned a degree based on its order relative to the first note of the scale, the tonic. Understanding degrees are crucial because it helps us understand the function of each note within the scale and its relationship and emotional quality to the tonic.

1st Degree (Tonic): The first note of the scale is called the tonic. It serves as the home base or central note. All other notes in the scale are measured in relation to the tonic. The tonic gives a sense of stability, rest, and resolution.

>   **Example:** In the C major scale (C, D, E, F, G, A, B), 'C' is the 1st degree or tonic.
>   **Emotional Sound:** Calm, stable, and resolved.

2nd Degree: The second note in a scale. This note creates a sense of tension, as it is a step away from the tonic, but it typically feels like it is leading somewhere.

>   **Example:** In the C major scale, 'D' is the 2nd degree.
>   **Emotional Sound:** Tension or anticipation.

3rd Degree: The third note in a scale. This note helps determine whether the scale is major or minor. In a major scale, the 3rd degree gives a bright, happy, or uplifting sound, while in a minor scale, the 3rd degree creates a more somber or melancholic feeling.

>   **Example:** In the C major scale, 'E' is the 3rd degree.
>   **Emotional Sound:** In major scales, bright, happy, or uplifting; in minor scales, sad or melancholic.

4th Degree: The fourth note in a scale. This note creates a sense of tension, as it is slightly away from the tonic but has a feeling of being "unstable," often wanting to resolve to the tonic or another stable degree.

>   **Example:** In the C major scale, 'F' is the 4th degree.
>   **Emotional Sound:** Suspense, yearning, or instability.

5th Degree: The fifth note in a scale. This is a very stable and powerful note, often called the dominant. It has a strong tendency to resolve back to the tonic, creating a sense of completion or resolution when it does.

>   **Example:** In the C major scale, 'G' is the 5th degree.
>   **Emotional Sound:** Powerful, strong, and resolved when it resolves to the tonic.

6th Degree: The sixth note in a scale. This note often brings a more mellow, contemplative sound. In a major scale, it can give a sense of longing or sweetness, while in a minor scale, it adds to the somber or introspective feel.

> **Example:** In the C major scale, 'A' is the 6th degree.
> **Emotional Sound:** Sweet, warm, or nostalgic.

7th Degree: The seventh note in a scale. This note has a strong feeling of tension, as it is one step below the tonic. It often creates a sense of wanting to resolve to the tonic, which is why it's commonly used in dominant chords.

> **Example:** In the C major scale, 'B' is the 7th degree.
> **Emotional Sound:** Tension, suspense, and anticipation (leading back to the tonic).

8th Degree (Octave): The 8th degree is the same note as the tonic, but one octave higher. This note brings the scale to completion and resolution, returning to the starting point of the scale.

> **Example:** In the C major scale, 'C' (one octave higher) is the 8th degree, or the octave.
> **Emotional Sound:** Completion, resolution, and stability.

Let's Review:
Degrees: Degrees refer to the specific position of a note within a scale, such as the 1st, 2nd, or 3rd note, and they help define the function and role of each note in the scale.
Emotional Sound: each degree provides a unique emotional sound.
Tonic: is the first note of the scale.

Patterns in Music

Patterns are found throughout music. They appear in rhythm, pitch, and harmony. Recognizing them helps both musicians and listeners make sense of what they hear. Patterns bring order to music, making it easier to understand, remember, and connect with emotionally.

Rhythmic Patterns
Rhythmic patterns are created through repeated beats or rhythms. Think of the steady pulse of the drums or the strumming pattern of a guitar, these repeating ideas set the groove and give listeners something familiar to follow. Changing a rhythmic pattern, especially in an unexpected moment, can shift the energy or mood of a piece.

Pitch Patterns
Pitch patterns involve the arrangement of notes in scales, melodies, or chords. For instance, the major scale follows a specific sequence of whole and half steps: whole, whole, half, whole, whole, whole, half. Recognizing such patterns makes melodies more predictable and easier to navigate.

Chord Patterns

Chord patterns, or progressions, are the repeated sequences of chords that shape a song's harmony. A well-known example in popular music is the I–IV–V progression (such as C–F–G in the key of C). These patterns create a sense of movement and resolution that listeners quickly come to expect.

Why Patterns Matter

Recognizing patterns in music creates structure and continuity. They provide a framework for composers, make learning and memorizing music easier for performers, and give listeners a sense of connection and familiarity. Patterns are what turn sound into music.

The Major Scale

This is where everything we've discussed so far starts to comes together. We'll be using the C Major scale as our example because it only contains natural notes: C, D, E, F, G, A, B.

Important: The rules we discuss regarding the C Major Scale apply to all other major scales, regardless of the starting/tonic note.

The Major Scale is the foundational scale from which all other scales are created. It consists of seven notes and contains only Perfect and Major intervals, giving it its happy, bright emotional quality.

P1		M2		M3	P4		P5		M6		M7	P8
C	C#/Db	D	D#/Eb	E	F	F#/Gb	G	G#/Ab	A	A#/Bb	B	C

Figure 32: Intervals related to the C MAjor scale

This pattern of intervals are commonly referred to in steps, Whole steps (W) and half steps (H). They are arranged in a specific order to form the major scale.

Interval Pattern of the Major Scale.
W – W – H – W – W – W – H (W = Whole step, H = Half step)

C	C#/Db	D	D#/Eb	E	F	F#/Gb	G	G#/Ab	A	A#/Bb	B	C
W	⟶	W	⟶	H	W	⟶	W	⟶	W	⟶	H	

Figure 33: Interval Patteren of the Major Scale

Important: As long as you follow this pattern of intervals, no matter what note you start on, you will always be playing the major scale for that note.

To construct a major scale, simply choose a starting note, the tonic, and apply the whole and half-step pattern to find the other notes in the scale. For example, starting on 'C' and applying this pattern, you get the C Major Scale: C, D, E, F, G, A, B.

As we progress, you'll notice that scales, through their specific patterns of intervals, are also associated with emotional qualities. The Major Scale typically produces a happy, bright sound, giving it a generally uplifting feel.

C Major - Intervals - Step Pattern

C	C#/Db	D	D#/Eb	E	F	F#/Gb	G	G#/Ab	A	A#/Bb	B	C
P1		M2		M3	P4		P5		M6		M7	P8
W	→	W	→	H	→ W	→	W	→	W	→	H	→

Figure 34: Interval Step Pattern of the Major Scale

Listed below are the major scales in order of the Circle of Fifths, which we will cover later. Notice how the highlighted notes follow the Major scale pattern of intervals just discussed. As previously stated, starting on any note and following the major scale pattern of intervals you'll always be playing the major scale for that note.

Intervals of the major scale: P1, M2, M3, P4, P5, M6, M7

The Major Scales

Interval	P1		M2		M3	P4		P5		M6		M7
C Major	C	C#/Db	D	D#/Eb	E	F	F#/Gb	G	G#/Ab	A	A#/Bb	B
G Major	G	G#/Ab	A	A#/Bb	B	C	C#/Db	D	D#/Eb	E	F	F#
D Major	D	D#/Eb	E	F	F#	G	G#/Ab	A	A#/Bb	B	C	C#
A Major	A	A#/Bb	B	C	C#	D	D#/Eb	E	F	F#	G	G#
E Major	E	F	F#	G	G#	A	A#/Bb	B	C	C#	D	D#
B Major	B	C	C#	D	D#	E	F	F#	G	G#	A	A#
F# Major	F#	G	G#	A	A#	B	C	C#	D	D#	E	F
C# Major	C#	D	D#	E	F	F#	G	G#	A	A#	B	C#
Ab Major	Ab	A	Bb	B	C	Db	D	Eb	E	F	F#/Gb	G
Eb Major	Eb	E	F	F#/Gb	G	Ab	A	Bb	B	C	C#/Db	D
Bb Major	Bb	B	C	C#/Db	D	Eb	E	F	F#/Gb	G	G#/Ab	A
F Major	F	F#/Gb	G	G#/Ab	A	Bb	B	C	C#/Db	D	D#/Eb	E

Figure 35: Interval Chart of the Major Scales

By altering the intervals of the Major Scale, you can build other scales that have their own unique emotional sound. As we continue, it's important to keep the foundational Major Scale in mind. Understanding a note's relationship to its major scale will help clarify terms such as major, minor, diminished and augmented.

The Minor Scales

The minor scale is another essential scale in Western music, it has a darker or sadder sound compared to the major scale. There are three main types of minor scales, natural minor, harmonic minor, and melodic minor. Each type of minor scale is created by altering the intervals of the major scale.

Natural Minor Scale

The natural minor scale is closely related to the major scale. It can be found by starting on the 6th degree of any major scale and continuing with the same sequence of intervals. In other words, if you begin a major scale on its sixth note, you'll hear the natural minor pattern. The natural minor scale is formed by flattening the major 3rd, 6th, and 7th degrees of the major scale. For example, comparing C Major and C Natural Minor, you'll see the major 3rd, 6th, and 7th are lowered to become minor 3rd, 6th, and 7th. Side note the C Natural Minor is the relative minor of E-flat Major.

C Major: P1, M2, M3, P4, P5, M6, M7, P8

C	C#/Db	D	D#/Eb	E	F	F#/Gb	G	G#/Ab	A	A#/Bb	B	C
P1		M2		M3	P4		P5		M6		M7	P8

Figure 36: Intervals of the Major Scale

C Natural Minor: P1, M2, m3, P4, P5, m6, m7, P8

C	C#/Db	D	Eb	E	F	F#/Gb	G	Ab	A	Bb	B	C
P1		M2	m3		P4		P5	m6		m7		P8

Figure 37: Intervals of the Minor Scale

Just as the major scale has a pattern of steps that make it easy to remember its intervals, so does the Natural Minor.

Interval Pattern of the Natural Minor Scale.
W – H – W – W – H – W – W (W = Whole step, H = Half step)

Major Pattern	W	→	W	→	H →W		→	W	→	W	→	H →
Minor Pattern	W	→	H →W		→	W	→	H →W		→	W	→
Degree	1		2	3← ③	4		5	6← ⑥	7← ⑦	8		
C Major Scale	C	C#/Db	D	D#/Eb	E	F	F#/Gb	G	G#/Ab	A	A#/Bb	B	C
C Minor Scale	C	C#/Db	D	Eb	E	F	F#/Gb	G	Ab	A	Bb	B	C

Figure 38: Interval Comparison Chart

To expand on the natural minor scale and its relationship with the major scale, let's analyze C Major and its relative minor the A minor.

Degree	1		2		3	4		5		6		7	8
C Major Scale	C	C#/Db	D	D#/Eb	E	F	F#/Gb	G	G#/Ab	A	A#/Bb	B	C

Figure 39: The 6th Degree of the Major Scale

Let's compare the notes of the C Major to the A minor.

The notes of C Major are: C, D, E, F, G, A, B.
The notes of A Minor are: A, B, C, D, E, F, G.

Starting on the 6th degree of the C Major scale and continuing upward gives us the notes of the A natural minor scale. This scale follows the interval pattern W–H–W–W–H–W–W (whole step, half step, etc.).

Now let's compare A Major with A minor. In A Major, the 3rd, 6th, and 7th degrees are in the Major position, the notes are C#, F#, and G#. In A minor, the 3rd, 6th, and 7th degree notes are in the minor position. Changing the notes to C, F, and G. This shift changes the sound of the scale from the bright, uplifting quality of major to the darker, more somber character of minor.

The notes of A Major are: A, B, C#, D, E, F#, G#.
The notes of A Minor are: A, B, C, D, E, F, G.

C Major Scale/Degrees Compare to Its Natural Minor (A) to the (A) Major																								
1		2		3	4		5		6		7	8		9		10	11		12		13
C	C#/Db	D	D#/Eb	E	F	F#/Gb	G	G#/Ab	A	A#/Bb	B	C	C#/Db	D	D#/Eb	E	F	F#/Gb	G	G#/Ab	A
Degrees of the A Scale									1		2	3← ③	4		5	6← ⑥	7← ⑦	8			
A Minor Scale									A	A#/Bb	B	C	C#/Db	D	D#/Eb	E	F	F#/Gb	G	G#/Ab	A
A Major Scale									A	A#/Bb	B	C	C#	D	D#/Eb	E	F	F#	G	G#	A

Figure 40: Comparison Chart of the Major & Minor Scales

28

Harmonic Minor Scale

The *harmonic minor* scale is derived from the natural minor scale by raising the 7th degree by a semitone (half step). This alteration creates an augmented second between the 6th and 7th degrees, giving the scale a distinctive exotic or dramatic sound, often described as "Eastern". This is a characteristic featured in classical music, particularly in Middle Eastern and flamenco styles.

Augmented Second

An augmented second refers to an interval that spans one and a half steps, or one whole step plus a half step. For example, in *A harmonic minor*, the interval between 'F' (6th degree) and 'G#' (7th degree) is an augmented second.

	P1		M2	m3	M3	P4		P5	m6	M6	m7	M7	P8
A Natural Minor Scale	A	A#/Bb	B	C	C#/Db	D	D#/Eb	E	F	F#/Gb	G	G#/Ab	A
A Harmonic Minor Scale	A	A#/Bb	B	C	C#/Db	D	D#/Eb	E	F	F#/Gb	G	G#	A

Figure 41: Comparison Chart of the Natural & Harmonic Minor Scales.

Interval Pattern of the Harmonic Minor Scale.
W – H – W – W – H – WH – H
(W = Whole step, H = Half step WH = One and a Half steps)

Melodic Minor Scale

The *melodic minor* scale is also derived from the natural minor scale, but has different rules for ascending and descending forms.

Ascending Melodic Minor:

When ascending, the 6th and 7th degrees of the Natural Minor scale are raised. This alteration brightens the scale and makes it smoother for melodic movement, often used in classical music.

Descending Melodic Minor:

When descending, the Melodic Minor scale reverts to the Natural Minor scale. This means the 6th and 7th degrees are flattened when descending, creating a more somber and stable sound.

Interval Comparison of the A Minor Variation

	P1		M2	m3		P4		P5	m6	M6	m7	M7	P8
A Natural Minor Scale	A	A#/Bb	B	C	C#/Db	D	D#/Eb	E	F	F#/Gb	G	G#/Ab	A
A Harmonic Minor Scale	A	A#/Bb	B	C	C#/Db	D	D#/Eb	E	F	F#/Gb	G	G#	A
A Melodic Minor Scale	A	A#/Bb	B	C	C#/Db	D	D#/Eb	E	F	F#	G	G#	A

Figure 42: Comparison Chart of the three Minor Scales

Let's Review:
Harmonic Minor Scale: Derived from the Natural Minor scale, by raising the 7th degree by a semitone.
Augmented Second: An augmented second refers to an interval that spans one and a half steps.
Distinctive Sound: The augmented second between the 6th and 7th degrees creates an exotic or dramatic sound.
Melodic Minor Scale: Also derived from the Natural Minor scale, but raises both the 6th and 7th degrees when ascending and returns to the natural minor when descending.

Understanding Modes

Modes are variations of a scale that begin on different degrees/note, of a scale. Though they contain the same notes within the scale, each mode creates a unique sound or character based on which note of the scale you start on and which intervals are emphasized. Think back to what we just discussed with the C Major and it relative A minor scales. The A minor scale is the *Aeolian mode* of the C Major scale.

We most commonly explore modes derived from the Major Scale (also known as the *Ionian mode*). We'll use the C Major scale for our example but remember that modes apply to all major scales. When we take the C Major Scale, which contains all natural notes (no sharps or flats), and begin on each successive degree, we create a different mode.

The C Major Scale: Foundation for Modes
The C Major Scale consists of the following notes: C – D – E – F – G – A – B – C

When we build modes from this scale, we retain the same notes but shift the starting point. Each new mode emphasizes different interval patterns and scale degrees.

Modes are a powerful way to expand your musical vocabulary. They allow you to create new emotional colors and moods without changing the notes you play, just the way you play them. By mastering the modes of the C Major Scale, you open the door to understanding modes in any key.

The Seven Modes of the Major Scale

Here are the seven modes that can be derived from the C Major Scale, starting on each degree:

Mode Name	Starting Note	Notes (from C Major)	Mode Type	Quality/Feel
Ionian	C	C – D – E – F – G – A – B	Major	Bright, happy, balanced
Dorian	D	D – E – F – G – A – B – C	Minor	Jazzy, soulful, mellow
Phrygian	E	E – F – G – A – B – C – D	Minor	Exotic, tense, Spanish
Lydian	F	F – G – A – B – C – D – E	Major	Exotic, tense, Spanish
Mixolydian	G	G – A – B – C – D – E – F	Major	Bluesy, rock-like, relaxed
Aeolian	A	A – B – C – D – E – F – G	Minor	Sad, reflective, natural
Locrian	B	B – C – D – E – F – G – A	Diminished	Dark, unstable, dissonant

Figure 43: Mode Cahrt

Next, we'll look at the interval patterns associated with each mode.

Interval Pattern

Each mode has its own *interval pattern*. Below is a chart outlining the unique interval patterns for each of the seven modes. While all modes are built using the same seven notes of the major scale, what makes each one distinct is the sequence of whole steps (W) and half steps (H) between the notes. These patterns shape the characteristic sound and mood of each mode, whether bright and stable like Ionian, or dark and tense like Locrian. Understanding these interval formulas is key to building and identifying modes starting on any root note.

Mode Name	Number	Interval Pattern	Mode Type	Quality/Feel
Ionian	I	W – W – H – W – W – W – H	Major	Pop, classical, folk
Dorian	II	W – H – W – W – W – H – W	Minor	Jazz, funk, modal rock
Phrygian	III	H – W – W – W – H – W – W	Minor	Flamenco, metal
Lydian	IV	W – W – W – H – W – W – H	Major	Film scores, fusion
Mixolydian	V	W – W – H – W – W – H – W	Major	Blues, rock
Aeolian	VI	W – H – W – W – H – W – W	Minor	Natural minor sound
Locrian	VII	H – W – W – H – W – W – W	Diminished	Experimental, unstable

Figure 44: Mode Chart

Scales Recapped

Scales are fundamental building blocks in music theory, serving as the foundation for melodies, harmonies, and chords. Understanding how to construct and use different scales gives musicians a versatile toolkit to create a wide variety of musical textures and emotional expressions.

Here's a recap of some of the core concepts we've covered:

1. Major Scale and Its Modes

The Major Scale is the foundational scale, providing the basis for many other scales and modes. It has a specific pattern of whole and half steps, which creates a distinct, bright, and uplifting sound.

Modes are scales derived from the major scale by starting on different degrees of the scale. Each mode has a unique pattern of intervals and offers a distinct sound or emotional quality. Some common modes are:

> **Ionian Mode** (Major scale itself)
> **Dorian Mode** (Minor scale with a raised 6th degree)
> **Phrygian Mode** (Minor scale with a lowered 2nd degree)
> **Mixolydian Mode** (Major scale with a lowered 7th degree)
> And others like Lydian, Aeolian (Natural Minor), and Locrian.

These modes provide a diverse palette for creating harmonic and melodic expressions in music, each contributing its own flavor and emotional color.

2. Minor Scales and Their Variations

The Minor Scale is often associated with a more somber, melancholic sound. There are three main types of minor scales:

> **Natural Minor (Aeolian mode):** Derived from the major scale by flattening the 3rd, 6th, and 7th degrees. It follows the interval pattern W-H-W-W-H-W-W.

Harmonic Minor: Derived from the Natural Minor scale, it raises the 7th degree by a semitone, creating an augmented second between the 6th and 7th degrees. This gives it a distinctive dramatic or Eastern sound with the interval pattern W-H-W-W-H-WH-H.

Melodic Minor: Also derived from the Natural Minor scale, but raises both the 6th and 7th degrees when ascending, and returns to the Natural Minor scale when descending. This makes it unique in having different ascending and descending forms. The ascending pattern is W-H-W-W-W-W-H.

3. Simplified and Altered Scales

Some scales are simplified by removing certain notes, making them more accessible or offering unique sounds.

Examples include:

Pentatonic Scale: A five-note scale that omits certain degrees of the major or minor scale to create a more open, accessible sound. The Major Pentatonic scale is typically the 1st, 2nd, 3rd, 5th, and 6th degrees of the major scale, and the Minor Pentatonic is derived from the natural minor scale by using its 1st, 3rd, 4th, 5th, and 7th degrees.

Blues Scale: Derived from the minor pentatonic scale but with the addition of a "blue note", which is typically a flattened 5th degree of the scale. This gives the Blues scale its distinctive, soulful, and expressive quality often used in blues music.

Conclusion

In conclusion, understanding scales and modes is crucial for any musician as it opens the door to creating a wide variety of sounds and emotions. Scales not only provide structure to melodies and harmonies but also enable musicians to evoke specific feelings, from the bright, joyful sound of the Major scale to the somber, reflective mood of the Natural Minor or the dramatic tension of the Harmonic Minor. Additionally, simplified scales like the Pentatonic and Blues scales offer musicians an accessible, expressive tool for genres like blues, rock, and pop.

By mastering the theory behind these scales, musicians can experiment with different moods, harmonies, and melodies, making their music richer and more versatile.

Chapter 6: Theory Applied - Chords

In this chapter, we'll explore the foundational concepts of chord writing and how it directly relates to scales. Understanding chords and their relationship to scales is essential for creating harmonies and progressions in music.

Just as scales provide a framework for melodies, chords provide the harmonic foundation. By selecting specific notes from a scale, we can form different types of chords such as major, minor, diminished, and augmented chords, each creating its own emotional effect. Additionally, applying modes and modifying the notes within a scale enables the creation of chords with various moods and styles.

Building Chords

Chords are built by stacking notes, typically in intervals of thirds, on top of a root note. This process begins with a scale as the source material, most commonly the major or minor scale. By selecting specific scale degrees and stacking them in a consistent pattern, we create the building blocks of harmony.

The most basic type of chord is the triad, which consists of three notes: the root, the third, and the fifth. More complex chords are created by adding additional scale degrees, such as sevenths, ninths to these triads.

Understanding how chords are built provides insight into how harmony works and sets the foundation for chord progressions, voice leading, and composition. Whether you're playing a simple folk tune or analyzing a jazz chart, chord construction is at the heart of musical structure.

Let's start by looking at the double stop.

Double Stops: The Simplest Chords

A *double stop* is the most minimal form of a chord. It's just two notes played simultaneously. While technically not a full chord, which requires three or more notes, double stops are harmonically significant and widely used in various musical styles, especially in string and guitar-based music.

Double stops are commonly used to:
- Outline a harmony without playing a full chord
- Add harmonic texture in solos or accompaniments
- Emphasize specific intervals, such as thirds, fifths, or sixths

Because they are composed of only two notes, double stops can be interpreted in multiple harmonic contexts. For example, a double stop of 'E' and 'G' could imply a C major chord (as the third and fifth), or an E minor chord (root and minor third), or other more complex harmonies, depending on the context.

Triads: The Foundation of Harmony

Triads are three-note chords made up of a root, a third, and a fifth. They are the fundamental units of Western harmony and are built by stacking two consecutive intervals of a third above a root note.

There are four primary types of triads:

Major triad: Root + Major third + Perfect fifth

Minor triad: Root + Minor third + Perfect fifth

Diminished triad: Root + Minor third + Diminished fifth

Augmented triad: Root + Major third + Augmented fifth

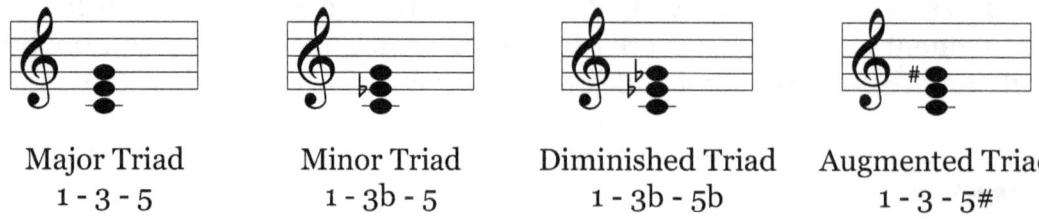

| Major Triad | Minor Triad | Diminished Triad | Augmented Triad |
| 1 - 3 - 5 | 1 - 3b - 5 | 1 - 3b - 5b | 1 - 3 - 5# |

Figure 45: Triads on the Staff

Triads form the basis for most harmonic progressions in classical, popular, and jazz music. Each type of triad carries its own emotional color and function within a key. Understanding how to build and identify triads is essential for interpreting chord symbols, composing, and improvising.

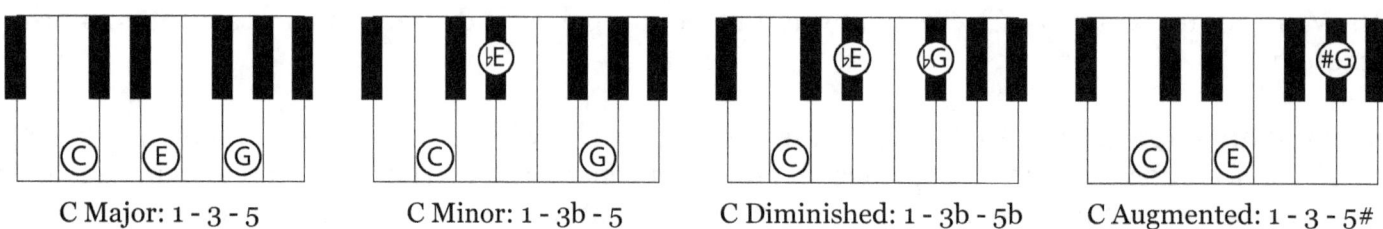

C Major: 1 - 3 - 5   C Minor: 1 - 3b - 5   C Diminished: 1 - 3b - 5b   C Augmented: 1 - 3 - 5#

Figure 46: Triads on the Piano

Extended Chords: Beyond the Triad

Extended chords are created by adding additional scale tones, usually in thirds, above the basic triad. These chords introduce richer, more colorful harmonies and are especially common in jazz, gospel, and contemporary styles.

The most common extended chords include:

Seventh chords (e.g., Major 7, Dominant 7, Minor 7)
Ninth chords (e.g., C9, Cmaj9, Cm9)
Eleventh chords (e.g., C11)
Thirteenth chords (e.g., C13)

These chords are formed by continuing to stack thirds from the root of the scale:

1st (Root), 3rd, 5th, 7th, 9th, 11th, 13th

Not all extended chords use every possible tone; often, some notes are omitted for clarity or ease of play. Additionally, tensions (e.g., 9, 11, and 13) can be altered (e.g., b9, #11) to create even more nuanced harmonic textures.

Extended chords allow for greater expressiveness and harmonic complexity. They open the door to more sophisticated progressions, voice leading, and modulation techniques.

Chord Inversions: Reordering the Harmony

Chord inversions occur when a note other than the root is played as the lowest (or bass) note of the chord. While the chord's identity remains the same, its sound, function, and voice leading can change significantly depending on which chord tone is in the bass.

Inversions are especially important for:
- Creating smoother bass lines
- Connecting chords with minimal movement
- Adding variety and interest to harmonic progressions

Triad Inversions

Triads have three possible positions:

Root position: The root is the lowest note (e.g., C–E–G)
1st inversion: The third is in the bass (e.g., E–G–C)
2nd inversion: The fifth is in the bass (e.g., G–C–E)

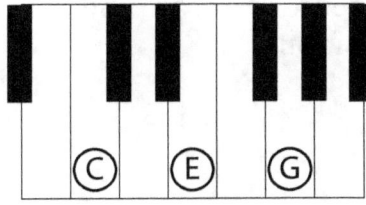 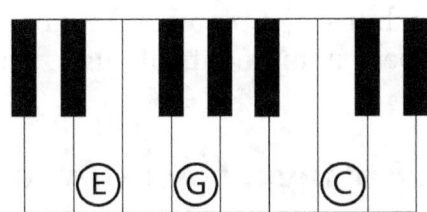 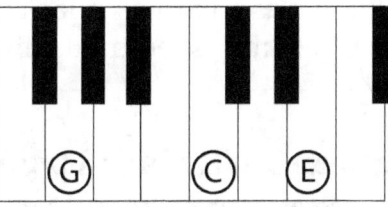

C Major Root: 1 - 3 - 5   C 1st Inversion: 3 - 5 - 1   C 2nd Inversion: 3 - 1 - 5

Figure 47: Triad Inversions

Seventh chords, which consist of four notes (root, third, fifth, and seventh), have four positions:

Root position: Root in the bass (e.g., C–E–G–Bb)
1st inversion: Third in the bass (e.g., E–G–Bb–C)
2nd inversion: Fifth in the bass (e.g., G–Bb–C–E)
3rd inversion: Seventh in the bass (e.g., Bb–C–E–G)

Chord Quality and Emotion: How Intervals Shape Feeling

Chords are more than just combinations of notes, they're emotional building blocks in music. The quality of a chord refers to its specific combination of intervals, particularly between the root, third, and fifth. These intervals create tension, resolution, or color, giving each chord a distinct emotional character.

Let's explore the four most common types of triads and the feelings they often evoke.

Major Triad: Bright, Happy, Stable

Structure: Root + Major third + Perfect fifth
Example: C – E – G
Sound: Strong, open, and uplifting
Common Emotion: Joy, triumph, confidence

The major triad is built with a major third (4 half steps) between the root and third, and a perfect fifth (7 half steps) from the root to the fifth. This structure produces a sound that feels complete and resolved. It's the foundation of countless songs in both classical and popular styles.

Minor Triad: Somber, Sad, Reflective

Structure: Root + Minor third + Perfect fifth
Example: A – C – E
Sound: Darker, more introspective
Common Emotion: Sadness, longing, tenderness

The *minor third* (3 half steps) gives this chord a more subdued and moody tone. Minor chords are often used to express emotion, depth, and vulnerability.

Diminished Triad: Tense, Unsettled, Mysterious

Structure: Root + Minor third + Diminished fifth
Example: B – D – F
Sound: Disorienting, suspenseful, unstable
Common Emotion: Anxiety, tension, drama

This chord narrows the space between the root and fifth, creating a *diminished fifth* (6 half steps), also known as a tritone. It lacks the stability of a perfect fifth, giving it a sense of unease and suspense. Diminished triads often appear in moments of tension or transition.

Augmented Triad: Dreamy, Strange, Unresolved

Structure: Root + Major third + Augmented fifth
Example: C – E – G#
Sound: Expansive, ambiguous, floating
Common Emotion: Surreal, mysterious, tension with elegance

The *augmented fifth* (8 half steps) gives this chord an unusual, "stretched" quality. It's symmetrical and doesn't strongly resolve to any key center, making it feel otherworldly or suspenseful. Augmented chords are used to color a progression or to transition into new harmonic areas.

Why Chord Quality Matters

Chord quality influences how music makes us feel and how we interpret a piece. By choosing different types of triads, composers and songwriters can convey a vast range of moods, even with just three notes.

As you continue studying chords, listen closely to how each type sounds. Try playing the same chord progression using different triad qualities, and notice how the emotional impact changes instantly.

Chords and Scales: Building Harmony from the Ground Up

Chords and scales are deeply interconnected. In fact, most chords in Western music are built directly from scales by stacking every other note (in intervals of thirds) starting on a given scale degree. This process reveals a natural harmonic structure within every key.

Chord Qualities in the Major Scale

When we harmonize a major scale, we can build a triad on each of its seven notes. The resulting chords follow a consistent pattern of major, minor, and diminished qualities:

Scale Degree	Note (in C major)	Chord Type	Roman Numeral
1st	C	Major	I
2nd	D	Minor	ii
3rd	E	Minor	iii
4th	F	Major	IV
5th	G	Major	V
6th	A	Minor	vi
7th	B	Diminished	Vii°

Figure 48: Chord Quality Chart

This pattern is true for every major key. So, in G major, for example, you'd find G major (I), A minor (ii), B minor (iii), C major (IV), D major (V), E minor (vi), and F# diminished (vii°).

Roman Numerals and Function

We use *roman numerals* to label chords based on their position in the scale. Uppercase numerals represent major chords, lowercase represent minor, and a degree symbol (°) denotes diminished chords.

Each degree has a typical function in a progression:

Tonic (I): Home base, stable, resolved
Subdominant (IV, ii): Moves away from tonic, prepares motion
Dominant (V, vii°): Creates tension, leads back to tonic

Common Chord Progressions in Major Keys

Certain combinations of chords appear frequently in music because of how their functions interact. These are called chord progressions, and they are the backbone of harmony.

Here are a few essential examples:

I – IV – V – I
One of the most common and stable progressions
Found in folk, classical, blues, and pop
In C major: C – F – G – C

ii – V – I
> Found frequently in jazz and classical music
> A smooth, strong resolution toward the tonic
> In C major: Dm – G – C

I – vi – IV – V
> The classic "50s progression" used in countless pop songs
> In C major: C – Am – F – G

vi – IV – I – V
> A more modern pop/rock pattern
> In C major: Am – F – C – G

I – V – vi – IV
> Another popular pop sequence (sometimes called the "Axis of Awesome" progression)
> In C major: C – G – Am – F

Why This Matters

By understanding how chords relate to the scale, you unlock the logic behind why music sounds the way it does. These patterns allow you to:

- Predict what chords might come next in a song
- Write your own chord progressions
- Understand the harmonic language of different musical styles

As you progress further in your quest to deepen your understanding of chords, you'll also encounter modal chord progressions, borrowed chords, and chromatic alterations, all of which stem from a solid grasp of how chords are built from scales.

<u>**Let's Review:**</u>
Chords: are built from scales by stacking intervals of thirds on scale degrees.
Double stops: are two-note harmonies, often used in string and guitar music to imply chords..
Triads: are the foundation of harmony and consist of three notes: the root, third, and fifth.
Chord inversions: rearrange the order of notes in a chord by placing a note other than the root in the bass, creating smoother transitions and varied textures.
Roman numerals: are used to label chords based on their position in the scale, helping to identify their function within a key.
Understanding chord construction and function helps musicians:
Write and analyze music
Improvise and compose harmonically rich pieces
Recognize patterns across different styles and genres

Chapter 7: Applying What You've Learned

From Theory to Application: Read It, Write It, Play It

Now that you've developed a solid understanding of scales, chords, and how they're built, it's time to turn that knowledge into skill. This section bridges the gap between theory and real-world application. The pages that follow are designed to help you reinforce what you've learned through active participation, reviewing concepts, writing them out, mapping them to your instrument, and listening closely to how each sound feels and connects.

Throughout this chapter, you'll find worksheets and guided exercises with space provided directly on the page. These activities are intended to be written in, allowing you to slow down, think critically, and physically engage with the material. Writing out musical concepts is a powerful learning tool and plays an important role in strengthening both understanding and retention.

To support your progress, a Practice Planner Worksheet is included to help you organize your practice sessions and reinforce a consistent Practice, Practice, Practice approach. By combining theory, repetition, and reflection, you'll develop greater confidence in both your musical knowledge and performance.

For readers who want additional practice, a companion workbook is available that expands on these exercises with extended drills and review pages designed to be used alongside this instructional text. A link and QR code are provided in this book for easy access.

Remember, as the saying goes, "When you love what you do, you'll never work a day in your life." The same applies to music, so enjoy the journey, and **Practice! Practice! Practice!**

How to Use the Practice Section

The Practice Section is designed to help you build a consistent, structured routine that mirrors the learning flow of this book. Start by using the Practice Planner Worksheet to schedule your sessions and outline what you want to focus on each day. A well-structured plan keeps your practice balanced, efficient, and intentional.

Each worksheet follows the same foundational sequence used throughout this book:

Music Notation, Reading & Writing Music

Begin each session by reviewing and practicing music notation. Strengthen your ability to read and write notes on the staff. This step sharpens your fluency and connects theory to written music.

Key Signature Memorization

Work through key signatures in order.

Start with identification, recognizing how many sharps or flats each key has.

Next, memorize the notes within each key signature.

Finally, memorize the chords that belong to each key.
This layered approach ensures deep understanding and instant recall when playing or composing.

Interval Practice

Develop your ear and spatial awareness by writing intervals on the staff, then finding those same intervals on the guitar neck and piano keyboard. This cross-instrument visualization reinforces how intervals look, sound, and feel.

Putting It All Together

Choose a key signature or scale, then write out its notes and chords. Map them onto the guitar and piano illustrations provided. This comprehensive step ties all your theoretical knowledge into one practical exercise, building true musical fluency.

Timing & Rhythm Development

Work with a metronome to improve timing, groove, and coordination. Start slow, then gradually increase tempo as you become comfortable. Focus on staying "in the pocket" and developing independent hand control, essential for smooth, confident playing.

Independent Practice Space

Use the blank staves, piano, and guitar illustrations for creative exploration. This is your space to experiment freely, compose short melodies, build new chord progressions, or practice any concept that inspires you.

By following this structure, you'll transform each practice session into a purposeful step forward. Consistency is key, stick with your plan, stay curious, and celebrate your progress. Over time, your understanding will become second nature, and your playing will reflect the depth of your study.

Ready? Turn the page and let's start applying everything you've learned.

Practice Planner Worksheet
Use this sheet to structure your daily practice sessions.

Date: _____

Goal for Today: (What are you focusing on? A specific scale? Chord shape? Song section?)

_____

_____

_____

1. Review (5 Minutes)
What did you learn last session? Write it, say it aloud, and refresh your memory.
Example: C Major scale formula (W-W-H-W-W-W-H), or review yesterday's riff.

Review Topic(s):

_____

_____

_____

2. Declarative Practice (10 Minutes)
Mental learning, away from your instrument. Study theory, notes, scale shapes, chord formulas, etc.
Write it out, say it aloud, and make sure you understand the "why."

Focus Concept:_____

Write what you learned below

_____

_____

_____

3. Procedural Practice (10 Minutes)
Muscle memory, with your instrument. Practice finger placement, accuracy, technique, and clarity.
Play it slowly and cleanly until you get it right 3x in a row, then speed up.

Skill / Exercise:_____

Did you play it clean 3x?   Yes   No (Try again tomorrow)

4. Free Play / Exploration (As Long As You Like)
Let loose! Improvise, write, or play a favorite song. Apply what you've learned.
What did you explore or enjoy today?_____

Reflections (Optional) What clicked today? What still needs work?_____

Cross out when complete: Review   Declarative   Procedural   Free Play

Staff Notation Practice Worksheet

This worksheet is designed to help you practice and internalize essential music reading and writing skills. As you move through each exercise, remember the proven learning method: Read it, Write it, Say it Aloud, and Repeat it. Consistent repetition will strengthen your understanding and help you recognize notation patterns more naturally.

Begin by using the staves below to practice drawing both the Treble and Bass clefs accurately. Start by copying the examples provided, then challenge yourself to draw them freehand. Continue practicing across the staff until each clef feels natural and easy to reproduce.

Focus on correct placement:
The Treble Clef (G Clef) circles around the G line, the second line from the bottom of the staff.
The Bass Clef (F Clef) uses two dots that frame the F line, the second line from the top of the staff.

Mastering these foundational symbols will make reading and writing music feel effortless. Take your time, stay consistent, and enjoy the process of building your notation fluency.

Notes on the Lines and Spaces

Write the names of the notes on the lines of the treble clef staff (from bottom to top):
E – G – B – D – F ("Every Good Boy Does Fine")

Write the names of the notes in the spaces of the treble clef (bottom to top):
F – A – C – E (spells "FACE")

Write the names of the notes on the lines of the bass clef staff (bottom to top):
G – B – D – F – A ("Good Boys Do Fine Always")

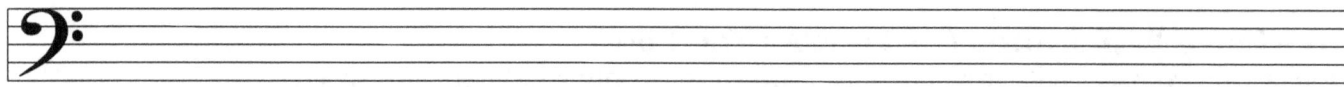

Write the names of the notes in the spaces of the bass clef (bottom to top):
A – C – E – G ("All Cows Eat Grass")

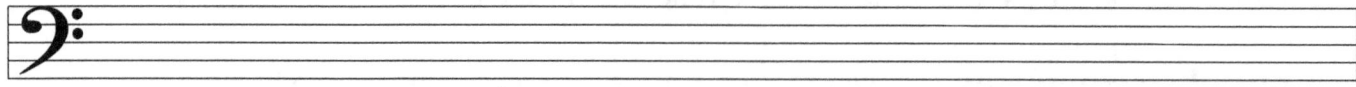

Time Signatures

A time signature tells you how many beats are in each measure and which note value receives one beat. On the staff below, write each of the following time signatures and label what each one means. Example: 4/4 = Four beats per measure; the quarter note gets one beat.

After writing each time signature, create one measure that correctly fits that rhythm. Use any combination of notes and rests as long as the total value matches the number of beats in the time signature.

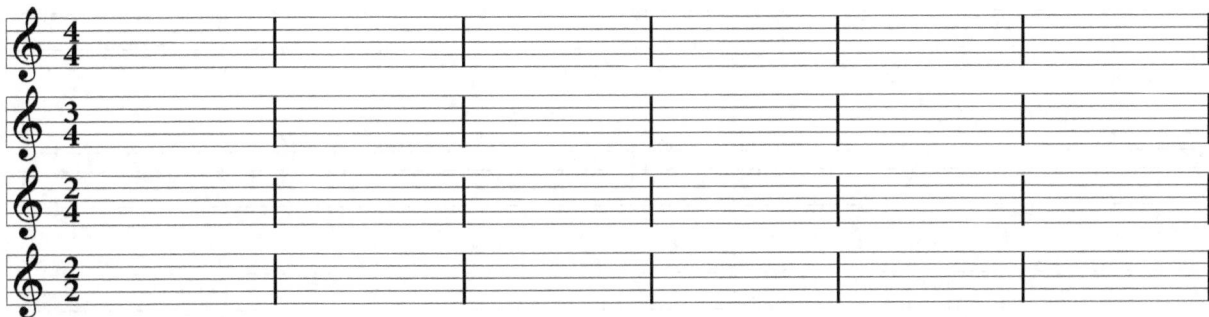

Notating Note Values

On the staff below, draw and label each of the following note types, then write how many beats each note receives in 4/4 time.

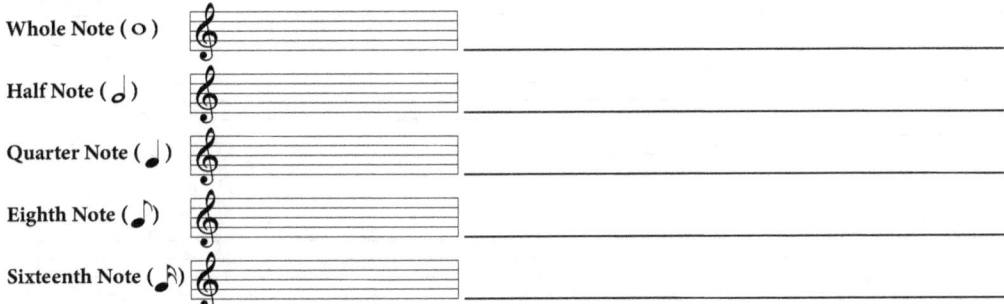

Notating Rest Values

Rests represent silence in music, just as important as the notes themselves. On the blank staff below, draw each of the following rest symbols, then write how many beats each rest receives in 4/4 time.

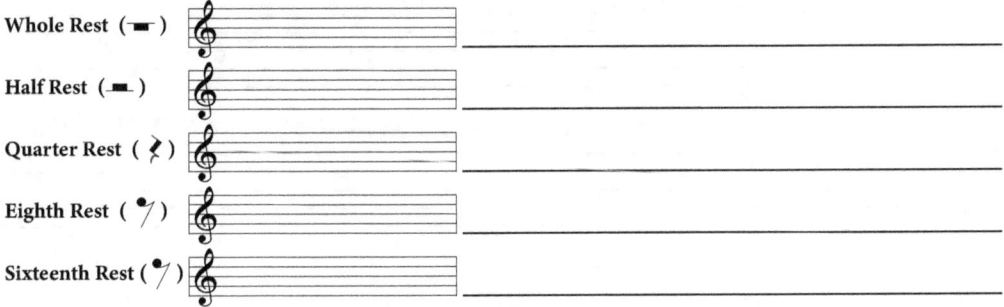

Read it – Write it – Say it aloud – Repeat.

Use the blank staves below for independent practice and creativity. Write scales, chords, melodies, or rhythm patterns of your own. This space is for exploring ideas, reinforcing what you've learned, and developing confidence in reading and writing music freely.

Key Signature Memorization Worksheet Instructions

How to Use This Worksheet
This worksheet is designed to help you memorize key signatures, one of the most essential foundations in music theory. Understanding key signatures allows you to instantly identify which notes are sharp or flat in any key, making reading music, writing scales, and building chords easier and more intuitive.

As with all concepts in this book, you'll follow the proven learning method:
Read it – Write it – Say it Aloud – Repeat it.

Step 1: Identify Key Names: Major and Minor Keys
In the first set of exercises, key signatures are already written on the staff. Your task is to write the name of the key (C, G, D, etc.) in the blank provided. As you work:

Say the key name aloud.
Double-check the sharps or flats for each key signature.
Repeat until recalling the key becomes automatic.

Step 2: Circle of Fifths: Counting Sharps and Flats
The Circle of Fifths is already provided with key signatures. Your task is to write the number of sharps or flats for each key in the blanks. This exercise reinforces both visual memory and conceptual understanding of key signature patterns.

Step 3: Key Notes Identification
For this section, the key signature is already written. Your task is to:

Identify the key.
Write the notes of the key in proper scale order (I, ii, iii, etc.) in the blanks provided.
This exercise reinforces your ability to connect a key signature to its corresponding notes and internalize scale structure.

Step 4: Key Chords Identification
Again, the key signature is already provided. Your task is to:
Identify the key.
Write the chords that belong to that key in the blanks provided.

This final step ties together key signature recognition, note memorization, and chord construction, giving you a complete understanding of how each key functions musically.

Why This Matters
By completing these exercises consistently, key signatures will become second nature. You'll strengthen both your declarative memory (knowing what's correct) and procedural memory (applying it automatically), allowing you to read, analyze, and write music confidently without hesitation.

Key Signature Memorization Worksheet

Major Key Signatures

Relative Minor Key Signatures

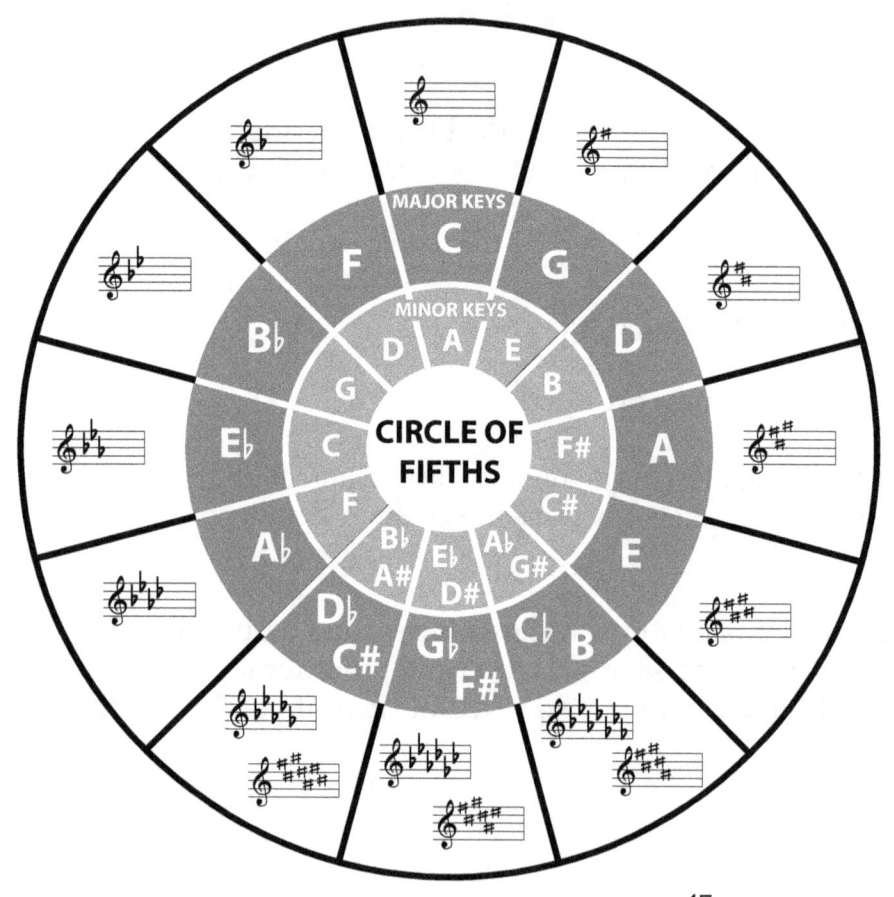

Write the number of sharps or flats next to each Scale/Key

C _____	F _____
G _____	Bb _____
D _____	Eb _____
A _____	Ab _____
E _____	Db _____
B _____	Gb _____
F# _____	Cb _____
C# _____	

Key Signature Identification & Scale Practice

Use this worksheet to practice identifying key signatures and writing out the notes that belong to each key. For each illustration, first look at the key signature and write the correct key name on the blank line labeled "Key Signature." Then, using the degree numbers provided below, fill in the corresponding notes of the scale that belong to that key, starting with the tonic (1st degree) and continuing through the 7th degree. Be sure to include any sharps or flats shown in the key signature.

Key Signature _____

I	ii	iii	IV	V	vi	vii°

Key Signature _____

I	ii	iii	IV	V	vi	vii°

Key Signature _____

I	ii	iii	IV	V	vi	vii°

Key Signature _____

I	ii	iii	IV	V	vi	vii°

Key Signature _____

I	ii	iii	IV	V	vi	vii°

Key Signature _____

I	ii	iii	IV	V	vi	vii°

Key Signature _____

I	ii	iii	IV	V	vi	vii°

Key Signature _____

I	ii	iii	IV	V	vi	vii°

Use this worksheet to practice identifying and writing scales for key signatures that contain flats. For each example, begin by examining the key signature and writing the correct key name on the line labeled "Key Signature." Then, using the degree numbers shown below, fill in the notes of the scale that correspond to that key, starting on the tonic (1st degree) and continuing through the 7th degree. Remember to include all the flats indicated in the key signature as you write each note of the scale.

Key Signature _____

I	ii	iii	IV	V	vi	vii°

Key Signature _____

I	ii	iii	IV	V	vi	vii°

Key Signature _____

I	ii	iii	IV	V	vi	vii°

Key Signature _____

I	ii	iii	IV	V	vi	vii°

Key Signature _____

I	ii	iii	IV	V	vi	vii°

Key Signature _____

I	ii	iii	IV	V	vi	vii°

Key Signature _____

I	ii	iii	IV	V	vi	vii°

Key Signature _____

I	ii	iii	IV	V	vi	vii°

Key Signature Identification & Diatonic Chord Practice

Use this worksheet to practice identifying and writing the diatonic chords within each key that contains sharps. Begin by looking at the key signature and writing the key name on the line labeled "Key Signature." Then, using the degree numbers provided, write the chord built on each scale degree, starting with the tonic (I) and continuing through the seventh degree (vii°). Be sure to include the correct accidentals as indicated by the key signature and use the proper chord qualities (major, minor, or diminished) for each degree.

Key Signature _____

| I | ii | iii | IV | V | vi | vii° |

Key Signature _____

| I | ii | iii | IV | V | vi | vii° |

Key Signature _____

| I | ii | iii | IV | V | vi | vii° |

Key Signature _____

| I | ii | iii | IV | V | vi | vii° |

Key Signature _____

| I | ii | iii | IV | V | vi | vii° |

Key Signature _____

| I | ii | iii | IV | V | vi | vii° |

Key Signature _____

| I | ii | iii | IV | V | vi | vii° |

Key Signature _____

| I | ii | iii | IV | V | vi | vii° |

Use this worksheet to practice identifying and writing the diatonic chords within each key that contains flats. First, examine the key signature and write the correct key name on the line labeled "Key Signature." Then, using the degree numbers shown, fill in the chords that belong to that key, starting with the tonic (I) and continuing through the seventh degree (vii°). Make sure to include all flats indicated in the key signature and label each chord with its correct quality (major, minor, or diminished).

Key Signature _____

  I   ii   iii   IV   V   vi   vii°

Key Signature _____

  I   ii   iii   IV   V   vi   vii°

Key Signature _____

  I   ii   iii   IV   V   vi   vii°

Key Signature _____

  I   ii   iii   IV   V   vi   vii°

Key Signature _____

  I   ii   iii   IV   V   vi   vii°

Key Signature _____

  I   ii   iii   IV   V   vi   vii°

Key Signature _____

  I   ii   iii   IV   V   vi   vii°

Key Signature _____

  I   ii   iii   IV   V   vi   vii°

Interval Practice Worksheet

Intervals are the building blocks of melody and harmony. This worksheet is designed to help you identify, write, and visualize intervals across multiple instruments, guitar and piano, as well as on the musical staff.

Use this page to reinforce your understanding of interval names, distances in half steps, and how they appear on your instrument. Practicing intervals helps improve your ear, your improvisation, and your understanding of scales and chords. Pair this with a metronome and your instrument for maximum effect.

Interval Reference Chart (Declarative Practice)

Interval Name	Semitones	Abbreviation	Example (C as root)
Unison	0	P1	C–C
Minor 2nd	1	m2	C–Db
Major 2nd	2	M2	C–D
Minor 3rd	3	m3	C–Eb
Major 3rd	4	M3	C–E
Perfect 4th	5	P4	C–F
Tritone	6	TT or A4/d5	C–F#/Gb
Perfect 5th	7	P5	C–G
Minor 6th	8	m6	C–Ab
Major 6th	9	M6	C–A
Minor 7th	10	m7	C–Bb
Major 7th	11	M7	C–B
Octave	12	P8	C–C (octave)

Using C for the root note, Here is an example of an exercise you can use to identify and memorize intervals. Simply, select a root note and write the intervals as demonstrated.

TIP: Intervals are counted from the tonic note (1st) to the target note (e.g., C to G = 5 = Perfect 5th).

Intervals on the Staff

Choose a root note and write a second note above it that corresponds an interval. Use whole notes and label the interval chosen (e.g., M3, P5, m6).

Example: Root note: C, Interval: Major 3rd, You write C and E

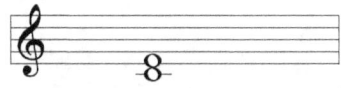

Root: C Interval: M3

Intervals on the Fretboard (Guitar-Focused)

Choose a root note and label it. Then write in the fret positions for different intervals (M3, P5, m7, etc.) from that root on the same string or across strings. This helps you visualize and memorize interval shapes.

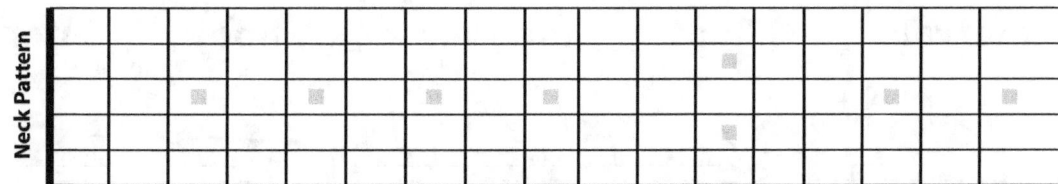

Tip: Use colored pencils to associate the intervals. Example: Root- Black, m3-Red, P5-Green.

Intervals on Piano Keys

Using the blank staff and keyboard diagram, select a root note and interval. Write the interval on the staff and mark the keyboard with the interval:

Root: ___ Interval: ___

Ear Training Ideas

Using your guitar or piano, play two notes back to back and name the interval. Start with a root note play the random second note and try and identify the interval. Once you believe you've identified the interval double check your answer by counting the semitones.

Another exercise is to sing the interval from a reference note. Don't worry how you sound. This is not a vocal exercise.

Interval Practice Blanks

Root: ___ Interval: ___   Root: ___ Interval: ___   Root: ___ Interval: ___

Root: ___ Interval: ___   Root: ___ Interval: ___   Root: ___ Interval: ___

Root: ___ Interval: ___   Root: ___ Interval: ___   Root: ___ Interval: ___

Root: ___ Interval: ___   Root: ___ Interval: ___   Root: ___ Interval: ___

Root: ___ Interval: ___   Root: ___ Interval: ___   Root: ___ Interval: ___

Fretboard Blanks

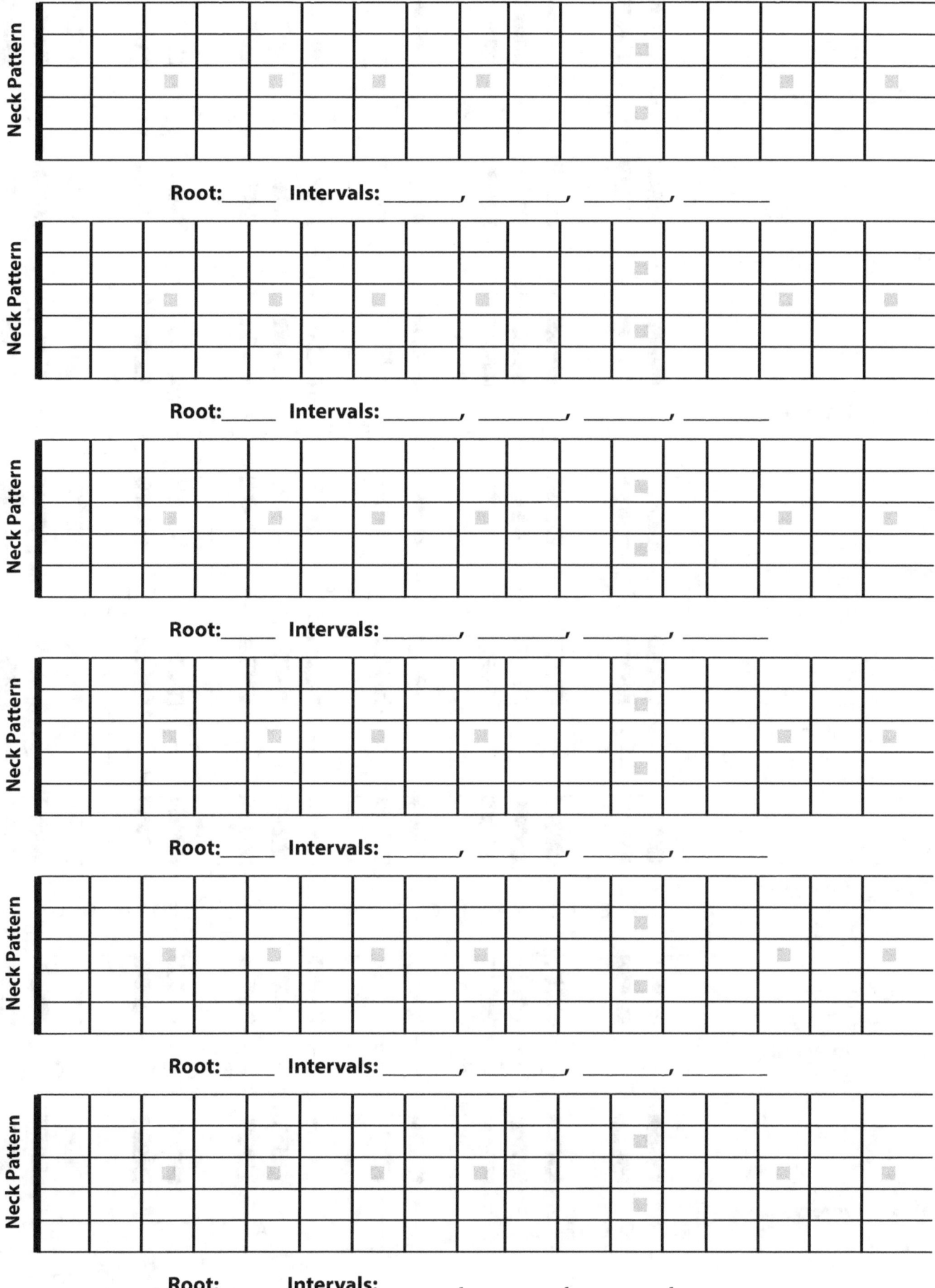

Neck Pattern

Root:_____ Intervals: _____, _____, _____, _____

Neck Pattern

Root:_____ Intervals: _____, _____, _____, _____

Neck Pattern

Root:_____ Intervals: _____, _____, _____, _____

Neck Pattern

Root:_____ Intervals: _____, _____, _____, _____

Neck Pattern

Root:_____ Intervals: _____, _____, _____, _____

Neck Pattern

Root:_____ Intervals: _____, _____, _____, _____

Piano Blanks

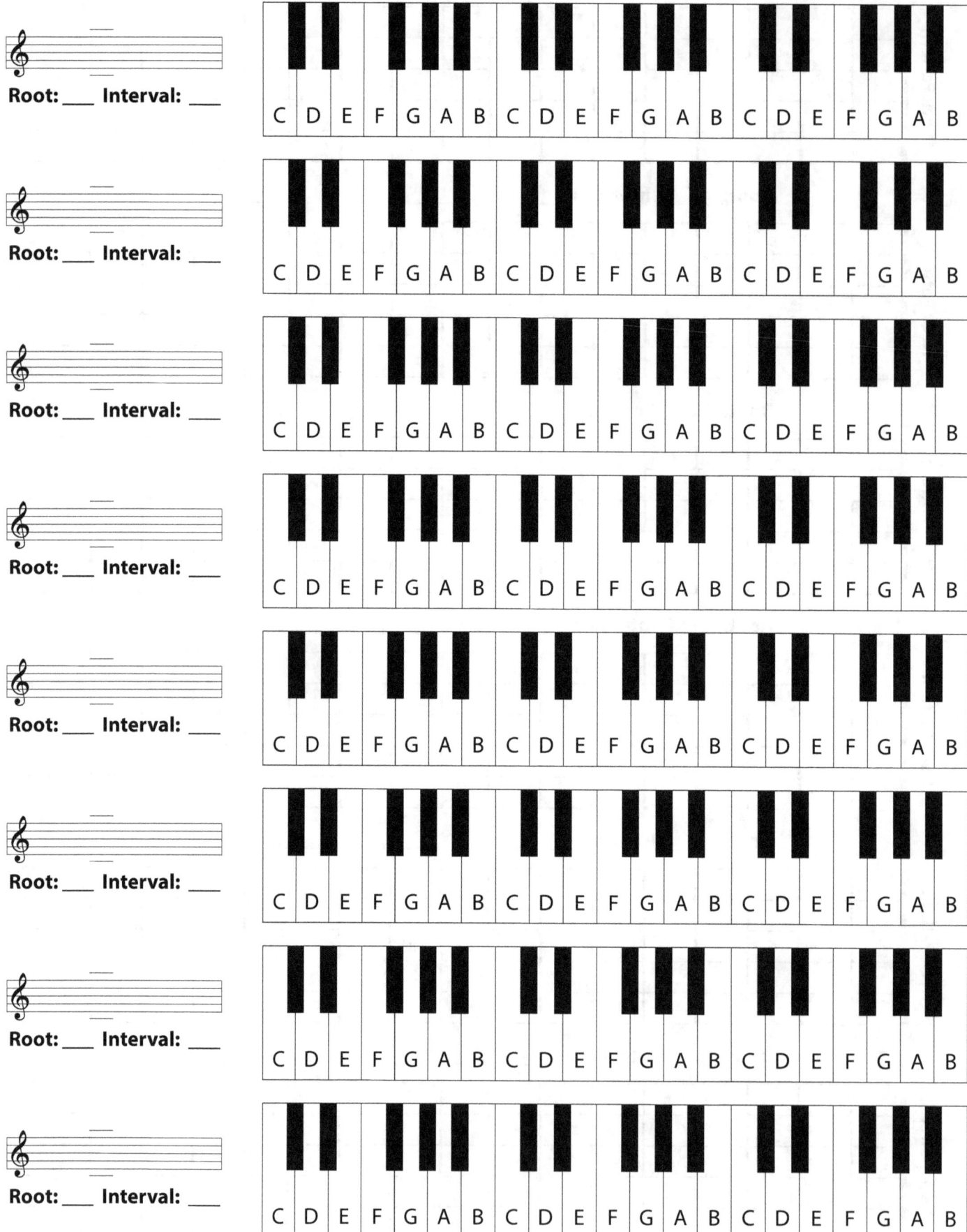

Scale/Chord Worksheet

This worksheet is designed to follow the same building block format as the book and reinforces the best practices for learning discussed earlier:

Read it. Write it. Say it aloud. Repeat.

Key Signature and Scale Notation

Start by selecting a scale (or tonic note). Write the corresponding key signature on the staff. This will help you quickly identify and recall key signatures.

Next, write out the notes of the scale on the staff. Say each note aloud as you write it. This helps reinforce your visual and auditory recognition.

Don't worry if you're unsure which note to use at first. This exercise is about improving your music reading fluency. With practice, you'll read music as naturally as you read a book.

Scale Structure & Chord Qualities

In this section, you'll write the interval pattern of the scale (e.g., W–W–H–W–W–W–H for major).

Then, write the notes of the scale, and memorize:
  The degree numbers (1st, 2nd, 3rd, etc.)
  The functional names (Tonic, Supertonic, Mediant, etc.)
  The modes associated with each scale degree (Ionian, Dorian, etc.)
  Lastly, identify the chord qualities for each degree (e.g., Major, Minor, Minor, Major, Major, Minor, Diminished). This is often referred to as the Chord Key.

Chord Names and Neck Visualization

Now identify the chord names built on each degree of the scale. Under each chord, you'll find a blank fretboard diagram.

Use these to identify and mark the notes that make up each chord. This helps you visualize how chords appear on the guitar neck, making it easier to apply them while playing.

Scale Mapping Across the Neck

This final section helps you memorize the notes across the guitar neck and understand how a scale moves across individual strings and the full fretboard.

Start with an open string (e.g., low E).
Identify its open note, then fill in the notes of the scale down the neck on that one string.
Repeat for each of the six strings.

As you work through all the strings, you'll begin to see patterns and visual shapes emerge that will help you navigate the fretboard with ease.

Pro Tip: Repeat until you can confidently recall the key signature, notes, intervals, chords, and their placement on the guitar without hesitation.

Scale/Chord Worksheet

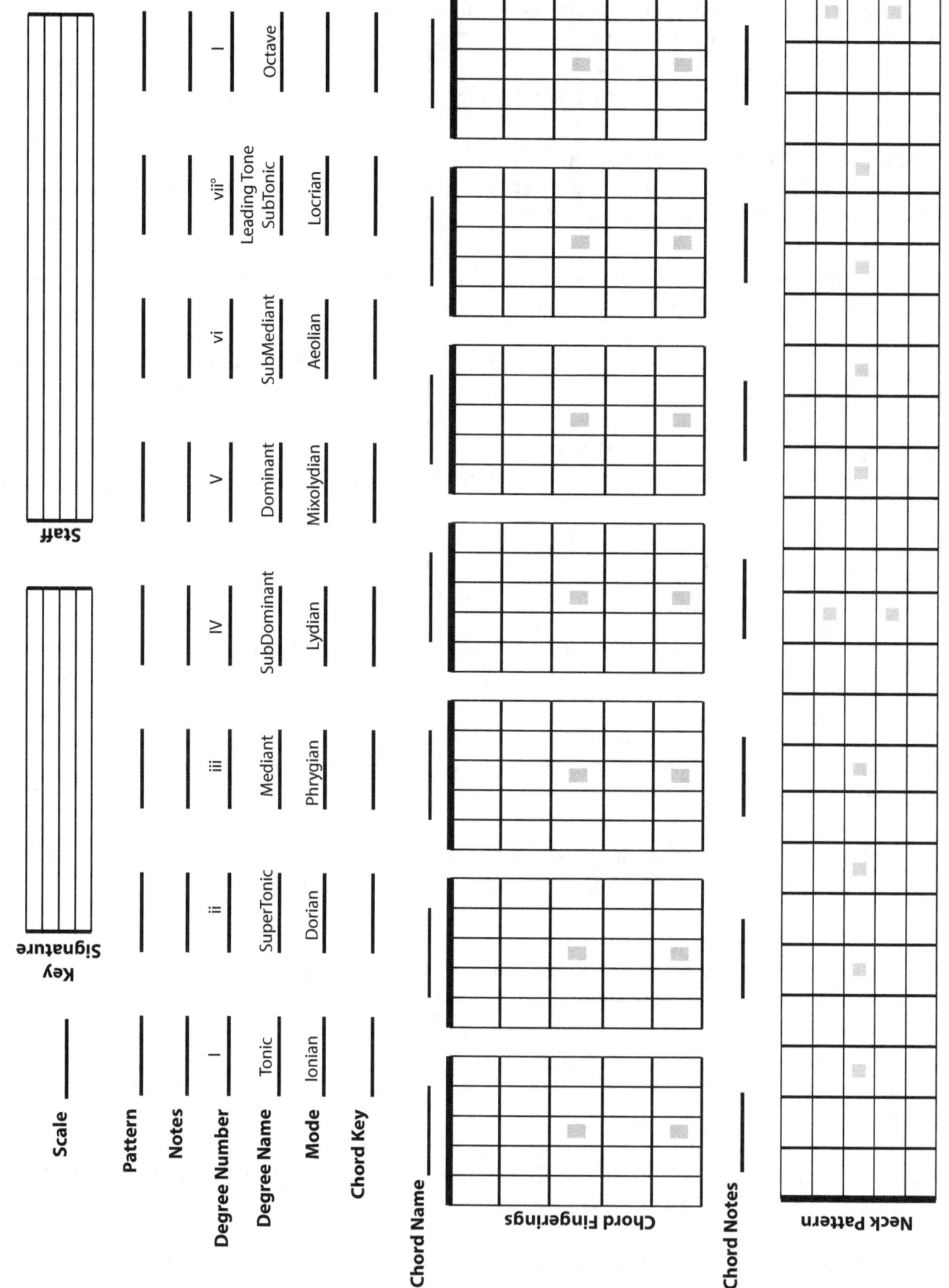

Staff

Key Signature

Scale ____

Pattern ____

Notes ____

Degree Number	I	ii	iii	IV	V	vi	vii°	I
Degree Name	Tonic	SuperTonic	Mediant	SubDominant	Dominant	SubMediant	Leading Tone / SubTonic	Octave
Mode	Ionian	Dorian	Phrygian	Lydian	Mixolydian	Aeolian	Locrian	

Chord Key ____

Chord Name ____

Chord Fingerings

Chord Notes ____

Neck Pattern

Scale/Chord Worksheet

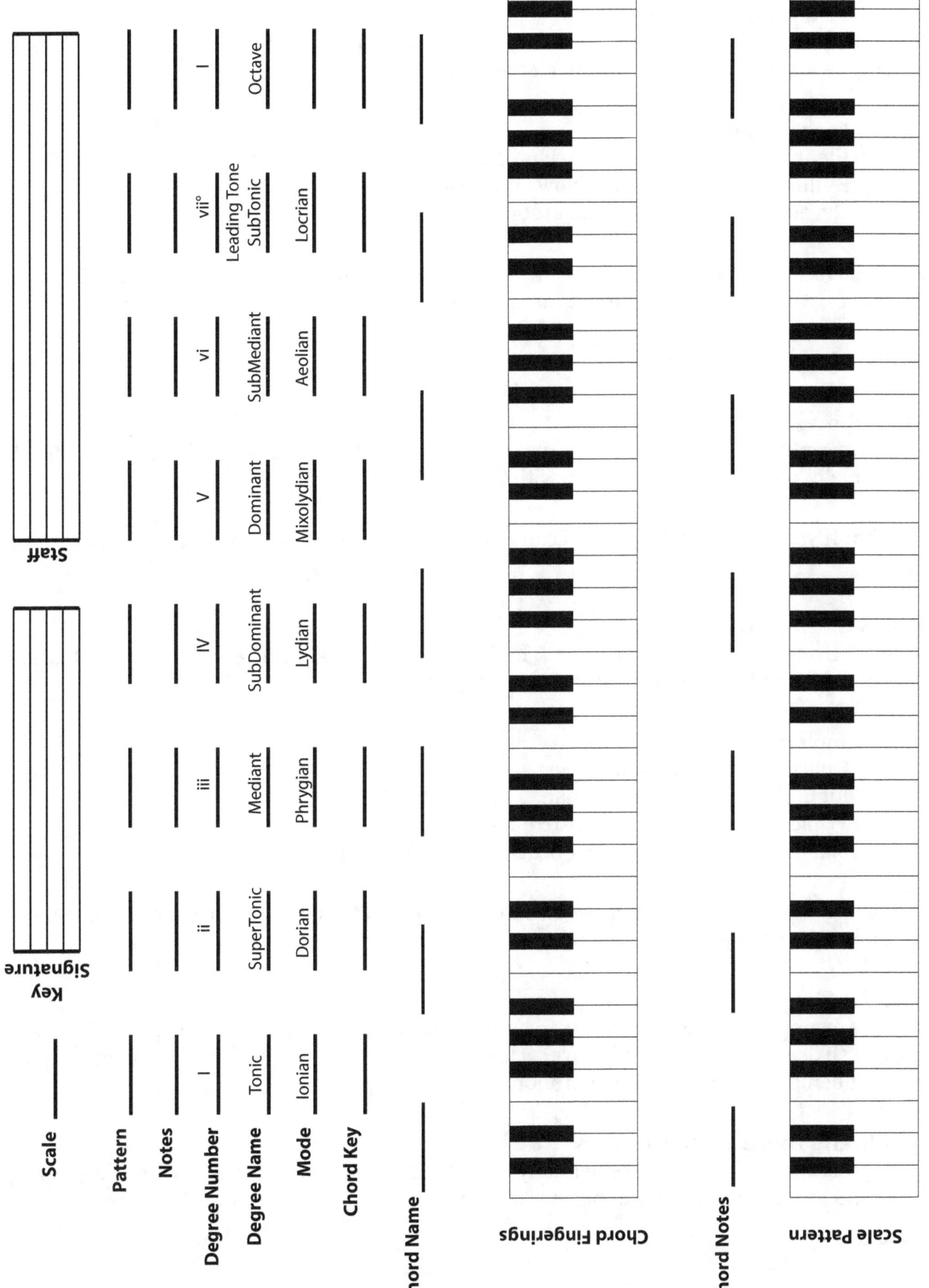

Staff

Key Signature

Scale ____

Pattern ____

Notes ____

Degree Number | I | ii | iii | IV | V | vi | vii° | I

Degree Name | Tonic | SuperTonic | Mediant | SubDominant | Dominant | SubMediant | Leading Tone / SubTonic | Octave

Mode | Ionian | Dorian | Phrygian | Lydian | Mixolydian | Aeolian | Locrian

Chord Key ____

Chord Name ____

Chord Fingerings

Chord Notes ____

Scale Pattern

58

Practicing with a Metronome

Why Use a Metronome?

Music is built on rhythm. You can hit all the right notes, but if your timing is off, everything falls apart. The metronome is like your personal timekeeper. It helps:

> Lock in your tempo
> Identify weak spots in your technique
> Build speed the right way (slow and steady)
> Develop internal timing and groove

Even the most expressive musicians have spent countless hours with a metronome. It's not just for beginners, it's for anyone serious about improving.

How to Practice with a Metronome

Start Slow

Choose a tempo (BPM, beats per minute) that is comfortably slow, even if it feels too easy. You want to be able to play cleanly and in time with the click.

Pro Tip: If you can't play it slow, you can't play it fast. Speed comes from control, not just moving faster.

Focus on Subdivisions

Most metronomes click once per beat. That's great for general timing, but many practice sessions benefit from subdividing the beat into smaller parts.

> Examples:
> Quarter Notes (1 click per beat)
> Eighth Notes (2 notes per beat: "1 & 2 & 3 & 4 &")
> Triplets (3 notes per beat: "1-trip-let, 2-trip-let...")
> Sixteenth Notes (4 notes per beat: "1-e-&-a, 2-e-&-a...")

Practicing your scales, riffs, or arpeggios to different subdivisions will give you a deeper sense of rhythm and improve your precision.

Use the "Less is More" Trick

Try this exercise: Set the metronome to half the speed you normally play. Let it click only on beats 2 and 4 (like a snare drum in a groove). This forces you to feel the groove internally and stay in time without being controlled by the metronome.

Gradually Increase the Tempo

Once you can play your exercise perfectly three times in a row at a certain tempo, bump it up by 2–4 BPM and repeat. Only increase the tempo when you're playing cleanly and in time.

Common Mistakes

Chasing the click: If you're constantly trying to "catch up" to the metronome, slow down and focus on staying centered in the beat.

Ignoring bad timing: If it sounds off, it is off. Don't settle for sloppy playing.
Going too fast too soon: Rushing progress leads to bad habits that are hard to brea

Memory Connection

Practicing with a metronome helps strengthen both: Procedural memory (muscle memory through repetition in time) and Internal rhythm awareness (developing an intuitive sense of groove)

Final Thoughts

The metronome isn't just a training tool, it's a mirror. It tells you exactly where your timing is strong and where it needs work. If you stick with it, your timing, confidence, and groove will improve dramatically.

Independent Hand Timing Exercise: Build Control. Strengthen Timing. Train Both Hands

When playing any instrument, especially piano, guitar, or drums. Developing the ability to use both hands independently and rhythmically is essential. Whether you're finger picking, chord switching, or playing melodies and bass lines together, both hands must stay in time, even when they're doing completely different things.

This exercise is simple and only requires:
A metronome
A sheet of paper (or use the chart provided)
Your left and right hands

Objective

To improve your ability to perform different rhythmic subdivisions with each hand, while keeping in time with a steady beat.

How It Works

Below is a simple timing grid. Each column represents one hand. Each row represents a number of hits (or taps) per beat.

Each number corresponds to how many taps per beat you'll perform. For example:

1 = one tap per beat (quarter notes)
2 = two taps per beat (eighth notes)
3 = triplets (three evenly spaced taps per beat)
4 = sixteenth notes (four taps per beat)

Left Hand	Right Hand
1	1
2	2
3	3
4	4

Step-by-Step Instructions
Set the metronome to a slow, comfortable tempo (around 60–70 BPM to start).

Start with both hands tapping once per beat (row 1). Tap your fingers or lightly drum on a table—just stay with the beat.

Once you're comfortable, keep your left hand tapping once per beat (still on row 1). Now, switch your right hand to row 2, tapping twice per beat while the left hand continues once per beat.

When that feels natural, switch your left hand to row 2 while the right hand stays.

Continue this process through all rows, practicing different combinations:

>   Left hand on 1, right hand on 3
>   Left hand on 2, right hand on 4
>   Left hand on 3, right hand on 1
>   And so on...

Why This Helps
This exercise works your procedural memory (muscle memory) and improves:
Hand independence
Subdivided rhythm awareness
Internal tempo control

It also helps you stay focused and calm under complexity, a skill that transfers directly into playing riffs, scales, and rhythms cleanly, especially when both hands are doing different things.

Left Hand	Right Hand
1	1
2	2
3	3
4	4

Notation Practice Worksheet

This worksheet is filled with blank staves designed for you to practice writing standard music notation by hand. Use these pages to work on note placement, key signatures, intervals, scales, chords, rhythms, or anything else you're studying. Handwriting music is a powerful way to strengthen your declarative memory, improve your understanding of music theory, and become more fluent in reading and writing music. Whether you're notating a scale, building chords, or copying a melody, this space is here for focused, hands-on learning.

Key Signature Memorization Worksheet - Answer Key

Major Key Signatures

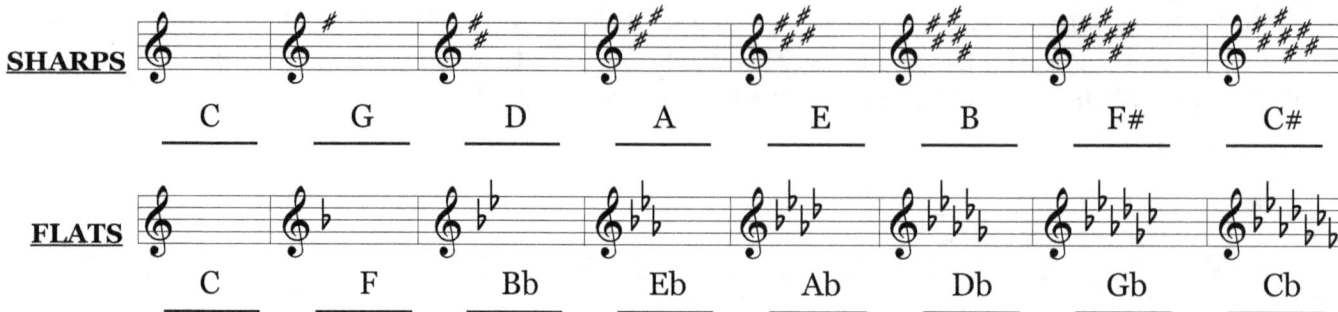

SHARPS

C   G   D   A   E   B   F#   C#

FLATS

C   F   Bb   Eb   Ab   Db   Gb   Cb

Relative Minor Key Signatures

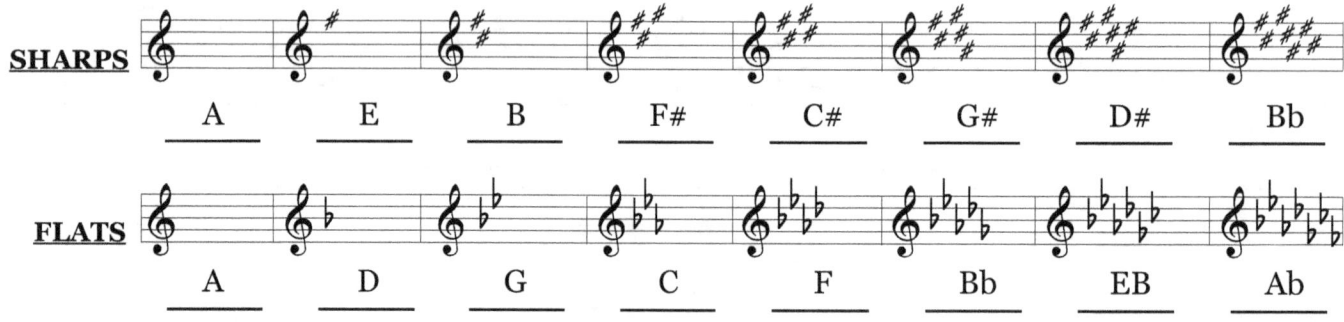

SHARPS

A   E   B   F#   C#   G#   D#   Bb

FLATS

A   D   G   C   F   Bb   EB   Ab

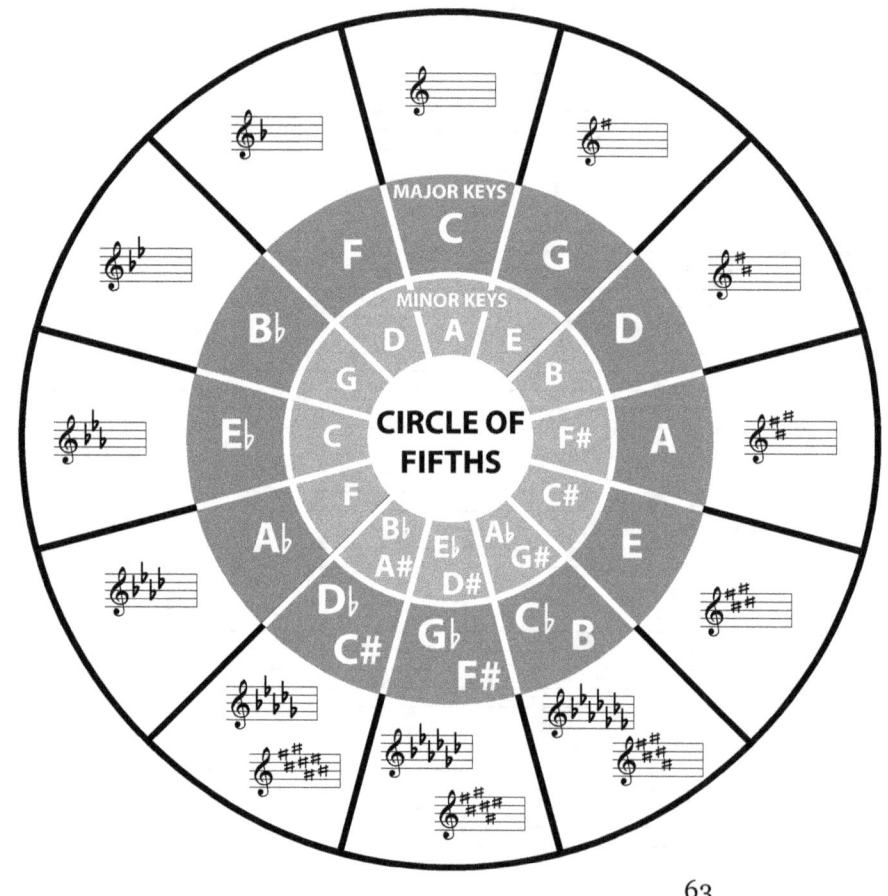

Write the number of sharps or flats next to each Scale/Key

C	0	**F**	1b
G	1#	**Bb**	2b
D	2#	**Eb**	3b
A	3#	**Ab**	4b
E	4#	**Db**	5b
B	5#	**Gb**	6b
F#	6#	**Cb**	7b
C#	7#		

Key Signature Identification & Scale Practice - Answer Key

Use this worksheet to practice identifying key signatures and writing out the notes that belong to each key. For each illustration, first look at the key signature and write the correct key name on the blank line labeled "Key Signature." Then, using the degree numbers provided below, fill in the corresponding notes of the scale that belong to that key, starting with the tonic (1st degree) and continuing through the 7th degree. Be sure to include any sharps or flats shown in the key signature.

Key Signature   C

C	D	E	F	G	A	B
I	ii	iii	IV	V	vi	vii°

Key Signature   G

G	A	B	C	D	E	F#
I	ii	iii	IV	V	vi	vii°

Key Signature   D

D	E	F#	G	A	B	C#
I	ii	iii	IV	V	vi	vii°

Key Signature   A

A	B	C#	D	E	F#	G#
I	ii	iii	IV	V	vi	vii°

Key Signature   E

E	F#	G#	A	B	C#	D#
I	ii	iii	IV	V	vi	vii°

Key Signature   B

B	C#	D#	E	F#	G#	A#
I	ii	iii	IV	V	vi	vii°

Key Signature   F#

F#	G#	A#	B	C#	D#	E#
I	ii	iii	IV	V	vi	vii°

Key Signature   C#

C#	D#	E#	F#	G#	A#	B#
I	ii	iii	IV	V	vi	vii°

Use this worksheet to practice identifying and writing scales for key signatures that contain flats. For each example, begin by examining the key signature and writing the correct key name on the line labeled "Key Signature." Then, using the degree numbers shown below, fill in the notes of the scale that correspond to that key, starting on the tonic (1st degree) and continuing through the 7th degree. Remember to include all the flats indicated in the key signature as you write each note of the scale.

Key Signature __C__

C	D	E	F	G	A	B
I	ii	iii	IV	V	vi	vii°

Key Signature __F__

F	G	A	Bb	C	D	E
I	ii	iii	IV	V	vi	vii°

Key Signature __Bb__

Bb	C	D	Eb	F	G	A
I	ii	iii	IV	V	vi	vii°

Key Signature __Eb__

Eb	F	G	Ab	Bb	C	D
I	ii	iii	IV	V	vi	vii°

Key Signature __Ab__

Ab	Bb	C	Db	Eb	F	G
I	ii	iii	IV	V	vi	vii°

Key Signature __Db__

Db	Eb	F	Gb	Ab	Bb	C
I	ii	iii	IV	V	vi	vii°

Key Signature __Gb__

Gb	Ab	Bb	Cb	Db	Eb	F
I	ii	iii	IV	V	vi	vii°

Key Signature __Cb__

Cb	Db	Eb	Fb	Gb	Ab	Bb
I	ii	iii	IV	V	vi	vii°

Key Signature Identification & Diatonic Chord Practice - Answer Key

Use this worksheet to practice identifying and writing the diatonic chords within each key that contains sharps. Begin by looking at the key signature and writing the key name on the line labeled "Key Signature." Then, using the degree numbers provided, write the chord built on each scale degree, starting with the tonic (I) and continuing through the seventh degree (vii°). Be sure to include the correct accidentals as indicated by the key signature and use the proper chord qualities (major, minor, or diminished) for each degree.

Key Signature C

C	Dm	Em	F	G	Am	Bdim
I	ii	iii	IV	V	vi	vii°

Key Signature G

G	Am	Bm	C	D	Em	F#dim
I	ii	iii	IV	V	vi	vii°

Key Signature D

D	Em	F#m	G	A	Bm	C#dim
I	ii	iii	IV	V	vi	vii°

Key Signature A

A	Bm	C#m	D	E	F#m	G#dim
I	ii	iii	IV	V	vi	vii°

Key Signature E

E	F#m	G#m	A	B	C#m	D#dim
I	ii	iii	IV	V	vi	vii°

Key Signature B

B	C#m	D#m	E	F#	G#m	A#dim
I	ii	iii	IV	V	vi	vii°

Key Signature F#

F#	G#m	A#m	B	C#	D#m	E#dim
I	ii	iii	IV	V	vi	vii°

Key Signature C#

C#	D#m	E#m	F#	G#	A#m	B#dim
I	ii	iii	IV	V	vi	vii°

Use this worksheet to practice identifying and writing the diatonic chords within each key that contains flats. First, examine the key signature and write the correct key name on the line labeled "Key Signature." Then, using the degree numbers shown, fill in the chords that belong to that key, starting with the tonic (I) and continuing through the seventh degree (vii°). Make sure to include all flats indicated in the key signature and label each chord with its correct quality (major, minor, or diminished).

Key Signature C

C	Dm	Em	F	G	Am	Bdim
I	ii	iii	IV	V	vi	vii°

Key Signature F

F	Gm	Am	Bb	C	Dm	Edim
I	ii	iii	IV	V	vi	vii°

Key Signature Bb

Bb	Cm	Dm	Eb	F	Gm	Adim
I	ii	iii	IV	V	vi	vii°

Key Signature Eb

Eb	Fm	Gm	Ab	Bb	Cm	Ddim
I	ii	iii	IV	V	vi	vii°

Key Signature Ab

Ab	Bbm	Cm	Db	Eb	Fm	Gdim
I	ii	iii	IV	V	vi	vii°

Key Signature Db

Db	Ebm	Fm	Gb	Ab	Bbm	Cdim
I	ii	iii	IV	V	vi	vii°

Key Signature Gb

Gb	Abm	Bbm	Cb	Db	Ebm	Fdim
I	ii	iii	IV	V	vi	vii°

Key Signature Cb

Cb	Dbm	Ebm	Fb	Gb	Abm	Bbdim
I	ii	iii	IV	V	vi	vii°

Scale/Chord Worksheet

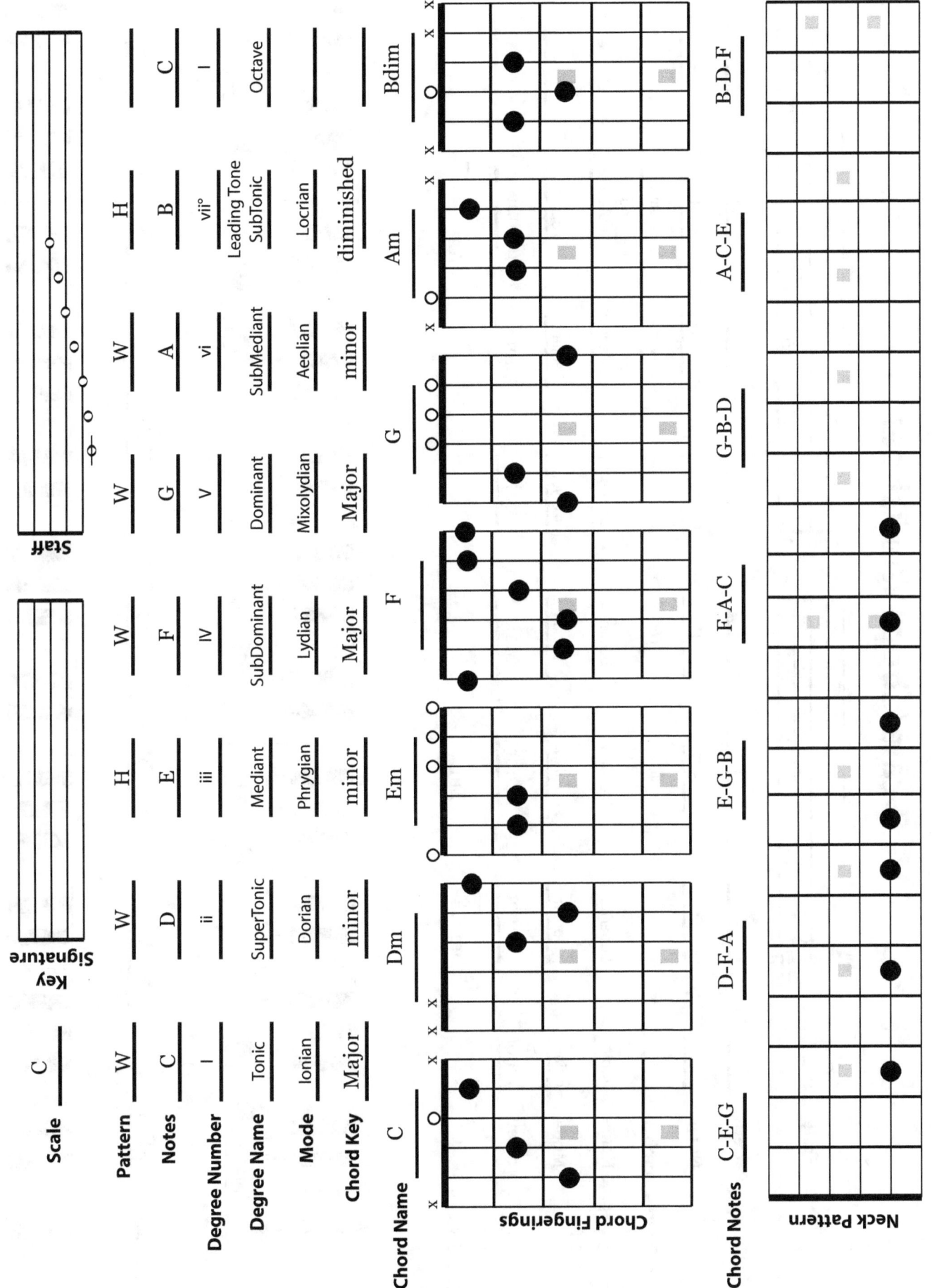

68

Scale/Chord Worksheet

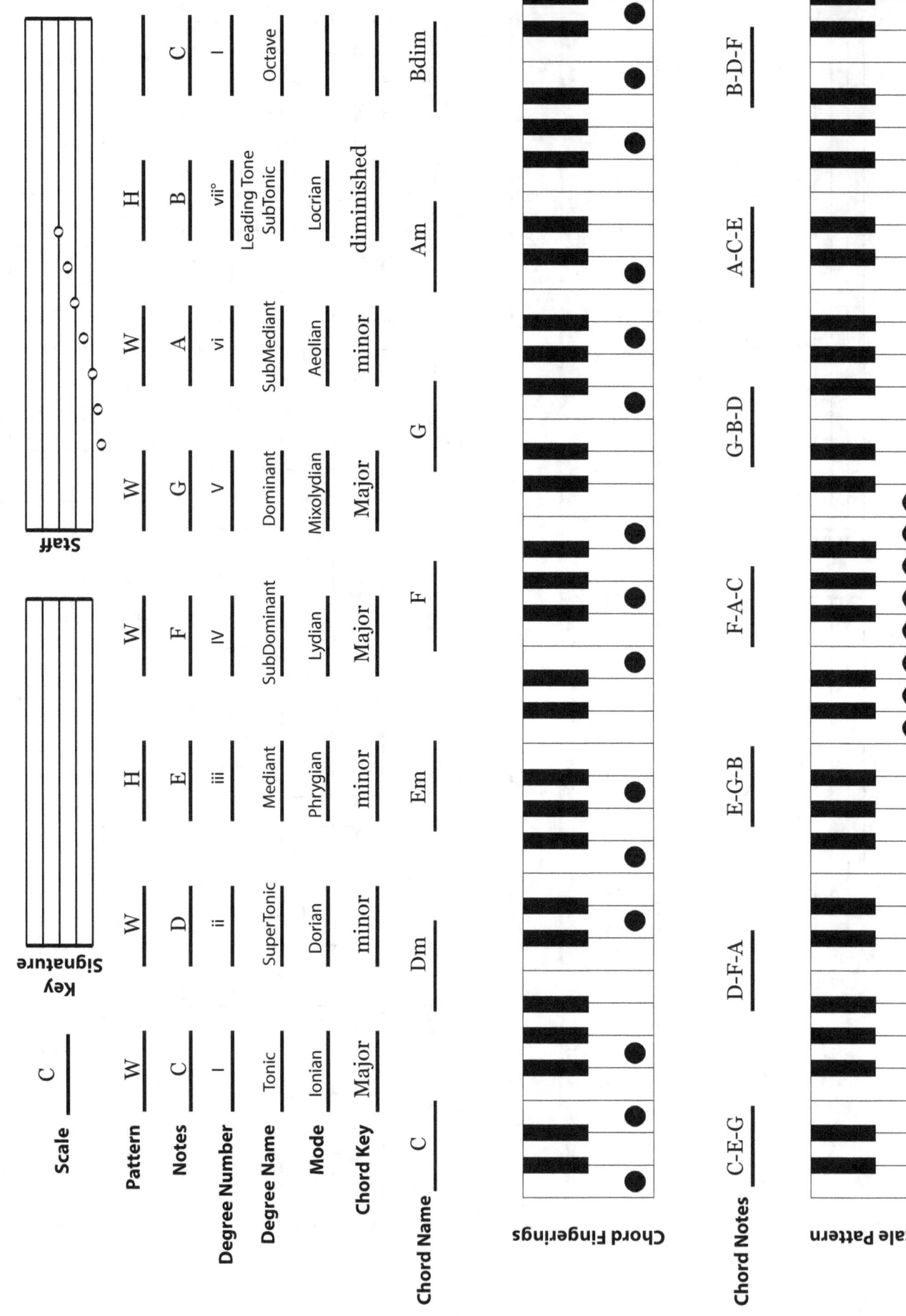

69

Glossary

General Music Terms

Note: A single musical sound or pitch.
Pitch: How high or low a note sounds.
Rest: A silence in the music.
Rhythm: Pattern of sounds and silences in time.
Tempo: Speed of the beat; measured in beats per minute (BPM).
Beat: The basic unit of time in music.
Meter: Grouping of beats, typically in 2s, 3s, or 4s.
Time Signature: Tells how many beats per measure.
Measure (Bar): A segment of time defined by a set number of beats.
Bar Line: A line separating measures.

Notation & Symbols

Clef: Symbol that indicates pitch range (e.g., Treble, Bass).
Staff (Stave): 5 lines on which music is written.
Ledger Lines: Extra lines for notes above/below the staff.
Sharp (#): Raises a note by a half step.
Flat (♭): Lowers a note by a half step.
Natural (♮): Cancels a sharp or flat.
Key Signature: Sharps/flats that define the key.
Accidental: A temporary sharp, flat, or natural.

Rhythmic Values

Whole Note: 4 beats in common time.
Half Note: 2 beats.
Quarter Note: 1 beat.
Eighth Note: ½ beat.
Sixteenth Note: ¼ beat.
Dotted Note: Adds half of the note's value.
Tie: Connects two same notes to extend duration.
Slur: Connects different notes smoothly.

Harmony & Scales

Interval: Distance between two notes.

Chord: 3+ notes played together.

Triad: 3-note chord: root, 3rd, 5th.

Seventh Chord: Triad + 7th interval.

Inversion: Reordering of chord tones.

Key: Tonal center of music (e.g., C Major).

Scale: Ordered sequence of notes (e.g., major, minor).
Arpeggio: Notes of a chord played separately.
Modulation: Changing from one key to another.
Cadence: Harmonic ending of a phrase (e.g., perfect, plagal).

Theory & Analysis
Tonic: 1st degree of a scale; home note.
Dominant: 5th degree; creates tension.
Subdominant: 4th degree; sets up dominant.
Motive: Short musical idea or theme.
Phrase: A musical sentence.
Period: Two phrases forming a complete thought.
Ostinato: Repeating rhythmic/melodic pattern.
Counterpoint: Interweaving independent lines.
Voice Leading: Smooth movement between chords.
Diatonic: Notes within a given key.
Chromatic: Notes outside the key.
Tritone: Interval of 3 whole steps; dissonant.

Articulation & Dynamics
Legato: Smooth and connected.
Staccato: Short and detached.
Accent (>): Emphasize the note.
Marcato (^): Stronger, marked accent.
Fermata (⌒): Hold the note longer.
Crescendo (cresc.): Gradually get louder.
Decrescendo/Diminuendo (dim.): Gradually get softer.
Forte (f): Loud.
Piano (p): Soft.
Mezzo Forte (mf): Moderately loud.
Mezzo Piano (mp): Moderately soft.
Fortissimo (ff): Very loud.
Pianissimo (pp): Very soft.
Subito: Suddenly (e.g., subito piano = suddenly soft).

Performance Directions
Allegro: Fast and lively.
Andante: Walking speed.
Adagio: Slow.
Largo: Very slow.
Presto: Very fast.

Ritardando (rit.): Gradually slow down.
Accelerando (accel.): Gradually speed up.
A tempo: Return to original tempo.
Rubato: Flexible tempo for expressiveness.
Da Capo (D.C.): Go back to the beginning.
Dal Segno (D.S.): Go back to the sign.
Fine: The end.
Coda: A separate, concluding section.

Slang/Informal Terms

Lick: A short melodic or rhythmic idea, often improvised.
Riff: Repeated phrase, often in rock/funk/blues.
Jam: Informal group improvisation.
Chops: Technical skill on an instrument.
Woodshedding ("Shedding"): Intense personal practice.
Groove: The feel or pocket of the rhythm section.
Head: Main theme or melody of a jazz tune.
Chart: Informal term for a lead sheet or sheet music.
Comping: Accompaniment style, usually in jazz.
Hook: Catchy part of a song, often the chorus or main riff.
Gig: A live performance.
Shed Session: Collaborative practice or jam time.
Vamp: Repeating a short progression or groove.

ABOUT THE PUBLISHER

3T Publishing is an independent publishing imprint focused on producing clear, practical learning resources for self-directed study.

Our publications are designed to present foundational subjects in a structured, accessible manner emphasizing understanding, application, and long-term retention. Each title is developed with clarity and usability in mind, making them suitable for independent learners, students supplementing instruction, and anyone seeking a well-organized introduction to a subject.

Learn more at:
3TPublishing.com

ABOUT THE AUTHOR

Rick Alexander is an independent author and publisher with a focus on creating structured, application-oriented learning materials.

His work emphasizes breaking down foundational concepts into clear, manageable steps, allowing readers to build understanding and apply what they learn with confidence. Through 3T Publishing, he develops instructional resources designed to support self-directed learning through clarity, structure, and practical examples.

www.ingramcontent.com/pod-product-compliance
Lightning Source LLC
Chambersburg PA
CBHW081723120626
46550CB00010B/3222